W9-BZU-252

2018 THE YEAR OF THE DOG AND THE MASTER

*This book is dedicated
to my friend and companion Balkahan,
who rescued me when I rescued him.
May he rest in peace
and reincarnate back to me soon.*

Half of the proceeds from this book
will be donated to dog shelters.

Gahl Sasson is an established author and has been teaching workshops on Storytelling, Kabbalah, Astrology, and Mysticism around the globe for over 20 years. His first book, *A Wish Can Change Your Life*, has been translated into over eight languages and is endorsed by HH the 14th Dalai Lama. His latest work, *Cosmic Navigator*, is the essential reference guide to understanding your astrological makeup.

He is a contributor to the Huffington Post, and Astrology. com, and has been named by W Magazine as one of "Los Angeles' Best Astrologer." Gahl was also chosen by Asia Spa Magazine as one of the 10 leading health practitioners in the world. His encyclopedic knowledge and charismatic presence have also made him a sought-after guest speaker. He is a guest lecturer at USC, Tel Aviv University, and teaches at Esalen, Omega Institute, University of Judaism, and the Open Center in NYC. He has appeared on CNN, ABC News, KTLA-TV Los Angeles to name a few. In 2017 his academic article, *Symbolic Meaning of Names in the Bible* was published by the Journal of Storytelling, Self, & Society. He currently resides in Los Angeles, but gives seminars and workshops regularly in USA, Argentina, Canada, Mexico, Russia, Lithuania, UK, Germany, Hong Kong, Spain, Singapore, Turkey, Israel, Bulgaria, and Switzerland. His web site is www.CosmicNavigator.com

GAHL E. SASSON

KIBEA

THE ASTROLOGY OF

The Year of the Dog and the Master

www.CosmicNavigator.com

*Special thanks to Kibea Publishing
for designing the book
and to Michael Davis' editing skills.*

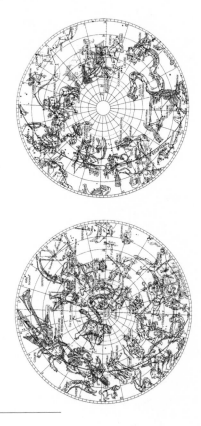

GAHL EDEN SASSON

THE ASTROLOGY OF 2018

contents

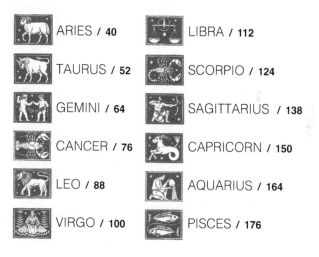

ASTROLOGY IS NOT A FORTUNE TELLING TOOL. It is a sophisticated system of symbols that explains the past, describes the present, and provides tools to design the future. Astrology is a GPS for the soul, a road map that helps us understand cycles. Astrology is the daughter of the ecstatic, passionate, and complicated relationship between Father Free Will and Mother Fate.

The heavenly bodies are part of the oneness that is creation. By looking at the orbits, transits, and aspects of the planets, we can better understand ourselves. All is One. The stars and planets do not influence us, but rather they correlate to our lives. They are the ginormous monitors and screens that reflect our lives, just as we are the tiny pixels that echo their own existence back to them. "As Above So Below", the alchemists assert and, indeed, whatever transpires in the upper worlds is mirrored in the here and now.

I hope these pages can serve as a cosmic map as you navigate the year 2018 and take your heavenly dog for a walk. Please remember that you are more than just your sun sign. You have a moon sign, an ascendant, and many other planets in your chart. However, your sign is like your spiritual tribe. The same way you read your local or national newspaper, you should read about your sun sign to inform yourself of your "local spiritual news." But please take time to read the introduction that explains the general trends of 2018 and not only the part that details what is expected for your sign. Reading the introduction will give you a deeper and better understanding of 2018, the Year of the Dog.

I wish you a happy and healthy year, full of abundance, creativity, love, and adventures. It is a wonderful thing to be a human and we are fortunate to have reincarnated during this
era at the dawning of the Age of Aquarius, the age of aware-
ness.

All is One. All is love.

I hope to see you in person in one of my lectures around the
globe.

GAHL,

City of Angels

		ARIES	♈
		TAURUS	♉
SUN	☉	GEMINI	♊
MOON	☽	CANCER	♋
MERCURY	☿	LEO	♌
SATURN	♄	VIRGO	♍
MARS	♂	LIBRA	♎
VENUS	♀	SCORPIO	♏
NEPTUNE	♆	SAGITTARIUS	♐
URANUS	♅	CAPRICORN	♑
JUPITER	♃	AQUARIUS	♒
PLUTO	♇	PISCES	♓

GENERAL GUIDELINES

RETROGRADE PLANETS

MARS

In Aquarius: 26th June – 13th August

In Capricorn: 13th August – 27th August

VENUS

In Scorpio: 6th October – 30th October

In Libra: 31th October – 16th November

MERCURY

In Aries: 22th March – 15th April

In Leo: 26th July – 18th August

SOLAR AND LUNAR ECLIPSES

31th January: Lunar eclipse

15th February: Solar eclipse

13th July: Solar eclipse

27th July: Lunar eclipse

11th August: Solar eclipse

part one

Introduction
to Cosmic Trends

2018

promises to be an explosive year. It is neither calm nor peaceful. It is like a hyperactive dog that can't stay still and needs long walks in the park. Well, that is an optimistic and nice way of looking at what is happening in the Year of the Earth Dog. We have 5 eclipses instead of the usual 4; we have 3 Mercury retrogrades; but we also have Mars retrograding for two months (June 26 – August 27) and Venus retrograding (October 6 – November 16). To make it even more complicated, we will have the last Mercury retrograde start right on the day Venus ends her retrograde motion. It means over two months of confusion and disarray. Also, the second eclipse this year falls right on the Chinese New Year (February 15). Whenever an eclipse occurs on a birthday or a beginning of a year, it makes the year far more volatile. To top it all, the year starts on a full moon. It is far more auspicious to bring something to a closure on a full moon, rather than begin.

If 2018 is the Year of the Dog, then we are talking about a pitbull rather than a docile poodle.

Numbers Tell Stories

In many languages, the word for "number" shares the same root or etymology as the word for "story". In English, I can ask my *accountant* to calculate my numbers and I can tell my partner an *account* of what has transpired at work. In Spanish, I can ask for *la cuenta*, my bill, but also *contar,* to tell a story. In Hebrew, a number is called *Mispar* (root SPR) and a story is *Sipur* (same root). These ancient truths embedded in many languages show that numbers are not only about quantity but also quality. They tell a story. This is of course the foundation of numerology. 2018 (2+0+1+8=11) adds up to the number 11. Usually in numerology, we reduce numbers above 9. For example, 2017 adds to 10 and then we reduce 10 to 1 since 1+0 is 1. However, there are a few numbers, like 22 and 11, that we do not reduce. They are called Master Numbers and carry a great deal of symbolism.

11 is made of two 1s. In Kabbalah, the mystical teaching of Judaism, creation is viewed as the mirror image of God. In other words, God created us in His/Her own image. Therefore 11 is the 1 looking at himself/herself in the mirror. 11 is the 1 who reflects upon the 1. Imagine yourself looking in the mirror. In reality, there is only one of you, but someone stand-

ing near by will see two images: you and your reflection. 11 teaches us that even if everything looks diverse and different, in reality there is only One. Since 11 is 1 looking at oneself, it is considered the most intuitive and mystical number. This year, do us all a favor. Trust your intuition!

But let's take a deeper look at 11. You can see it is made of two 1s, which indicates duality. 11 is connected to 2 and therefore to relationships - You and Me. 2018 is a very important year for relationships and love. Many of us will reassess our partnerships in work and/or in life. It is a year where our "significant others" will be scrutinized and reevaluated. Many of us will experience break-ups, especially around the eclipses (January 31, February 15, July 13, July 27, August 11), during Mars retrograde (June 26 to August 27), and during Venus Retro (October 6 to November 16). But, at the same time, many of us will reconnect to old partners or find new ones. Alas, some will both separate and then find a new love. The reason is fourfold:

Eclipses always quicken processes and in 2018 we have an extra eclipse, which is mostly in Leo, the sign of love. The eclipse on July 27/28 actually falls on Tu BeAv, the biblical day of love, celebrated from the time of the temple in Jerusalem.

This year we have both Venus (planet of love) and Mars (planet of passion and fights) in retrograde. Many break-ups and quarrels happen during retrograde motions.

The numerology of the year 2018 (11 and 2) puts an energetic focus on relationships and on the oppositions of "I versus thou" or "mine versus yours" and "me versus us".

In the Chinese astrology, 2018 is the Year of the Dog (starts February 15). The dog, more than any other animal, has the longest and deepest *relationship* with humans. Research shows that dogs were the first animal to be domesticated (some studies show they domesticated themselves). Don't be surprised if your partner or lover will try to domesticate you and make you a good well-tamed "puppy".

To conclude, 2018, being a Master Number, is a Master Year. Every dog needs an alpha or a master. It is a year when you could attract, harmonize, and understand relationships. These relationships could be in love, business, or leisure (partners in yoga, hobby, cycling, or shopping). In addition, this year affords you the opportunity to become a master in some (or a few) aspects of your life. This is the year to drill, to repeat, to be disciplined, to rehearse, and to complete your 10,000 hours of mastery. By the end of the year, when you look at the mirror, just like the 1 does in 11, you will be able to see you have grown, changed, and enhanced yourself. But remember that to be a master you have to go through the Dark Forest, dive into the Underworld, and tame the wild beasts, your inner "night-walkers".

Paradoxical Master

2018 begins with an end. It sounds like a paradox, but you better get used to contradictions since this is a paradoxical year. 2018 commences with a full moon in Cancer. The full moon represents an end, a completion. When the moon is full on Jan 1, it teaches the lesson of Ouroboros, the snake that bites its own tail, the symbol of infinity, no beginning, no end. It resonates the teaching of the Kabbalistic Sefer Yetzirah: the end is embedded in the beginning, the beginning in the end.

This is a year of alchemy, a year when oppositions can unite. After all, it is a Master Year or 11. Last time a year started on a full moon was 1999, the year we were all terrified would be our last (the 2YK paranoia). What it means, astrologically speaking, is that in order to start anew, we need to let go of the past. This year is a year in which we need to throw out the old to make room for the new. But it also means we need to accept contradictions and be able to contain paradoxes. We must realize that even when things appear to be in conflict or opposites, in reality, they are two different manifestations of the same oneness. It is the true message of relationships: two people who are opposite but the same.

New Year's Resolution – When and Why

New Year's is the only truly scared holiday on this planet. It is the only absolute holy day. While Christmas, Ramadan, Hanukkah, Vesak, Utsava, Yule, etc., are culturally relative holy days—that is, conditioned, and therefore limited, by faith, religion, or location—New Year's is the only sacred day that is celebrated by atheists and believers alike around the world.

I am very fortunate to teach in Istanbul, mother of cities, which for the last 500 years has been predominately Muslim. But on New Year's, the streets are glowing with bright festive lights and the trees are adorned with billions of LCD lights. My family and friends in Israel, mainly Jewish, also celebrate New Year's and adhere to the traditional midnight countdown. My friends in Los Angeles, mainly Christians, also celebrate the arrival of the new year. My colleagues in Hong Kong, mostly Buddhist, also send each other Happy New Year greetings. Indeed, this beautiful festival is celebrated all over the globe with a kiss and a hug. What a wonderful holiday! A true Earth celebration from New Zealand to Norway, Japan to the US, Finland to Argentina. No matter where you are on the planet, you, your friends and family, your cellphone and computers will switch from 2017 to 2018 with a big bang and a splash. Arguably, New Year's is the most popular celebration on the planet and how beautiful is the fact that it is sealed with a countdown 10,9,8…1 and then a kiss! Practically a numerological ritual, you invoke all the 10 archetypes and then you join lips with a kiss and a hug. Sometimes, I just love us human beings...

Janus, the Roman god of portals and namesake of January, is a perfect symbol for New Year's. Like the god's image, we spend New Year's splitting our consciousness between reviewing what we experienced in 2017 and projecting and envisioning what we wish to experience in 2018. January 1 is an energetic vortex. Therefore, on Jan 1, try to do a few symbolic acts that represent what you want to focus on in 2018. The first day of the year, as well as the first week of Jan, is the overture of the year ahead when you play the melodies of what you wish to hear later. For example, if your new year resolution is relating to love, then do something that represents relationships on the first day or week of the year. If it is a new diet, then eat healthy on Jan 1.

The best time to decide what your New Year's resolution will be is on December 31 (unless you are too drunk) and reflect upon it on Jan 1 (unless you have a hangover). But to actually start the process, wait until the day after the first New Moon of the year, which is Jan 16/17, depending on where you are on the globe. You can also use the energetic swell of the Chinese New Year, which starts on the New Moon of Aquarius, the sign of wishes, February 15.

狗 The Year of the Dog: Wagging its Tail from February 15

You might not follow or believe in Chinese Zodiac, but the fact that as many as 2 billion people do put their faith and destiny in the animal wheel makes it real. Since so many people will project a dog into the astral realm, one can conclude that in the collective unconsciousness there is going to be a huge dog barking and demanding to go on a cosmic walk.

2018, as we saw, is an 11 year and the dog is indeed the 11th branch of the Chinese zodiac. After all, a dog needs its master. Generally speaking, the Year of the Dog is about loyalty, bravery, protectiveness, honesty, spending time in the outdoors (dogs need long walks) but also nesting (dogs love lying on a sheepskin by the fireplace). It is a conservative and somewhat pessimistic year, which is supported by the fact that in Western Astrology, Saturn, the Lord Karma, moves into Capricorn, the conservative pessimistic sign of tradition.

This year, pay attention to dogs and try to connect to our canine friends. If you don't have a pooch and you have always wanted one, then this is the year you should adopt a furry friend. In the USA, there are around 76 million dogs. In 2018 you can join the dogling gang. As a person who had both dogs and cats, I can tell you from experience that while cats teach us how to give love unconditionally, dogs show us how to receive unconditional love. Kabbalah means *to receive*. We all need to learn receiving!

Feng Shui Colors for the year: Green, Red, Purple. To better channel the year's blessings, try to incorporate these colors in your clothes, home, and office design.

 ## Eclipses –
One Extra Lunation in 2018

"Is it good or is it bad?" many people ask. "It is not good or bad", I tend to answer. "It just is".

It is through a remarkable synchronicity that the solar disk is 400 times bigger but also 400 times farther than the moon. It makes their surfaces appear to have the same size when viewed from earth. It is a heavenly reminder that the feminine (moon) and masculine (sun) are equal. It is a metaphor, a cosmic poem, showing us that reception (moon) is just as important as action (sun) to achieve our goals.

Eclipses happen when the path of the moon crosses the path of the sun during a new or full moon. This happens usually four times a year (March and September in 2016; February and August in 2017). However, in 2018 it will happen five times.

Eclipses are wild-cards. They are unpredictable, like a hurricane. They amplify whatever process is currently happening in your life. That is the reason many people experienced such an intense period during February and August, 2017. Eclipses resemble a race car driver hitting the accelerator while taking a curve. The eclipses from 2017 until 2019 are in Leo and Aquarius (with the exception of July 13, which is in

Cancer). Since Leo rules love, romance, happiness, entertainment, sports, heart, spine, and Aquarius governs, friends, governments, colorations, circulatory systems, and sheens, these aspects in life or parts of your body are more emphasized. To make it more concise: the eclipses focus us on love and children (real children as well as the children of our mind) as well as friends and community. This series of eclipses happened before in 1998/1999 and in 1980/1981. Remember that astrology takes us to the past in order to create the future. Try to see what happened to you in those years (mistakes or good choices) so you can navigate and create the year ahead in a better way.

 The eclipse on July 13 is in Cancer and therefore, July will be colored with issues relating to home, family, motherhood, cars, real-estate, and a sense of security.

Eclipses are also storytellers and use synchronicities to shape the narratives of our lives. Since eclipses quicken processes, they push us into crossroads, demanding choices and decisions. A hero/heroin is determined by the choices he or she makes and so are we. Eclipses are junctions, crossroads that are made of endless synchronicities weaved together. Around eclipses, you will experience many more coincidences and serendipities. The eclipses occur on specific days (dates below), but their sphere of influence or radiation can be felt a week before and after. However, their stories unfold for six months.

Wherever the eclipse is visible, it has more power. Each eclipse also has what is called *Sabian* symbol. Every degree of the zodiac has an image that was channeled in 1925 by the clairvoyant Elsie Wheeler. These images and metaphors are very popular among astrologers around the world and I also find them to be helpful:

 January 31 – Total Lunar Eclipse. Full Moon in Leo. It takes place 11 degrees Leo, which is an interesting synchronicity considering that it is the year of 11. Symbol: An evening lawn party. Visible: North/East Europe, Asia, North/East Africa, North/West South America.

 February 15 – A day after Valentine's Day and right on the Chinese New Year. You better not forget your Valentine's and make sure you have reservation for a good restaurant! It is a Partial Solar Eclipse and a New Moon in Aquarius. Symbol: A tree cut or sawed. Visible: South of South America and Antarctica (expect a great number of icebergs to melt or fall off).

 July 13 – Partial Solar Eclipse. New Moon in Cancer. This eclipse is the only one that is outside the Leo/Aquarius group. It relates to home, real-estate, mother, security, nurturing, and vehicles. Symbol: A prima donna singing. Visible: South of Australia.

 July 27/28– Total Lunar Eclipse. Full Moon in Aquarius. It is also the biblical day of love. Symbol: A council of ancestors/elders. Visible: Much of Europe, Asia, Australia, and Africa. South America.

August 11 – Partial Solar Eclipse. New Moon in Leo. Symbol: A houseboat party. Visible: North/East Europe, North/West Asia, Greenland.

A week before and after these dates, you might feel more emotional, reactive, and sensitive. There is a reason why the mythical werewolves transform into beasts during the lunation. During the eclipses, we become more instinctual and less governed by reason. Our animalistic side takes control of us, and therefore it allows our wounded inner-child to come to the surface. Be strong in those periods for yourself as well as for the people around you. Knowing these astrological trends make you more responsible. You are reading these pages so that you can become a lighthouse for others as well as for yourself.

Mercury Retrograde – The Trickster

Three times a year for about three weeks, Mercury, the planet of communication, appears to travel backwards. Of course, the planet does not really retrograde, but he appears to do so from the viewpoint of an earthling. Since Mercury is the planet that governs business, travel, connections, computers, communications, contracts, trade, and transactions, these aspects of our lives experience a great deal of hardships. It is not recommended that you sign any documents, get married or engaged, make big purchases, start important projects, or publish during these periods.

People belonging to the signs that host Mercury while it is retrograding experience the effects of the retrograde motion more intensely. True to the explosive nature of 2018, this year Mercury is retrograding in fire signs (Aries, Leo, Sagittarius). Misunderstanding can burst into flames and small issues can accelerate into all-raging wars. Please take extra care during the periods listed below.

But it is not all darkness and gloom. During Mercury retrograde, it is a good time to edit, make plans for future ventures, revisit old abandoned projects, and reconnect with people you might have not seen for a while. It is also a good time to find lost objects.

March 22 – April 15,
Mercury retrogrades in Aries.

July 26 – August 18,
Mercury retrogrades in Leo.

November 16 – December 6,
Mercury retrogrades in Sagittarius and Scorpio.

Jupiter in Scorpio

From October 10, 2017 until November 7, 2018, Jupiter, the planet of expansion, luck, flow, and opportunities, is traveling in Scorpio. Of course, it is great news to Scorpio but also to Cancer and Pisces, fellow water signs and therefore, Water-Benders. It is also beneficial to Capricorn and Virgo, the earth signs or Earth-Benders. But Taurus should be a bit careful not to over-strain themselves, as Jupiter in Scorpio, their opposite sign, can create situations of over-commitment, and over-optimism.

According to the *Astrology of Becoming*, (see my book, *Cosmic Navigator*) even if you are not a Scorpio, you can still benefit from Jupiter's gifts in 2018 by "becoming" a Scorpio. You can embody the positive qualities of Scorpio, thus attracting the gifts that Jupiter bestows on the sign throughout 2018. How to become a Scorpio? Be deep, intense. Allow transformation to come into your life. Create intimate meaningful relationships. Shine your sexuality (without endangering yourself or anyone around you). Let go of things that are dead in your life so new ones can resurrect. Be a therapist when asked for advice, and allow your own healing to take place. Help others connect to their talents, and support other people's projects. Be less talkative, and listen more. Become an agent and manger for people around you. Allow magic into your life, and take active interest in the occult. Investigate, do a lot of research, and go to the root of problems. These qualities can build in you the energetic receptors for the celestial vibes of Jupiter in 2018.

From November 7, the energy shifts as Jupiter moves to his own sign, Sagittarius. That is great news to everyone, since Jupiter in Sagittarius is generous and fun-loving. It means lots of travel, adventures, luck, synchronicities, and flow in the last two months of the year.

Mars Retrogrades in Aquarius and Capricorn: June 26th to August 27th

The fatal and regrettable Brexit referendum took place during the last time that Mars was retrograding in Aquarius, the sign of government and community. And what happened right after? Oops, regret. What have we done? That is typical Mars retro reaction.

Mars is action. It can be implosive, passionate, and explosive. Mars gives us energy, assertion, leadership abilities, and the power to move mountains. It is associated with seeds and vegetation. When Mars is retrograding, it is not a very auspicious time to start big projects with large investments. It is not a good time for surgery and medical procedures. Neither is it recommended to start an intimate or sexual relationship. Avoid buying big machinery, making large investments, or starting wars or lawsuits. It is a more dangerous time, since wars, conflicts, explosions, and terror seem to follow Mars. After all, Mars' moons are called Phobos (fear) and Deimos (terror). If you need to fight, let the opponent shoot the first bullet. Whoever starts a war in Mars Retro, loses.

Mars retrograde affects everyone but mostly people with strong emphasis in Aries and Scorpio (sun sign, ascendant, moon). Since Mars is retrograding in Aquarius and Capricorn, these signs will also feel the heaviness of this aspect. Especially take heed between July 26 to August 18, when not only Mars but Mercury is retrograding. Miscommunications and misunderstandings can easily flare into full-fledged wars.

 Mars retrograde in Aquarius between June 26 until August 13: Conflict with friends, colleagues, governments, changes in leadership in companies, corporations, and countries.

 Mars retrograde in Capricorn between August 13 to August 27: Conflict with authority figures, bosses, frustration in career, strife with father figures.

Venus Retrograde in Scorpio and Libra: October 6th to November 16th

When Venus is retrograding, relationships of all types as well as our finances experience challenges and reversals. Venus retrograde happens for 40 days every 18 months. Since Venus rules Taurus and Libra, these signs are more sensitive to this aspect. Because Venus is retrograding in Scorpio (and Libra), people born under Scorpio will also share some of the burden of this retrograde motion.

When Venus is retrograde, it is not recommended to get engaged or married, form business partnerships, buy art, make investments, start lawsuits, or spend money. It is a time to reevaluate your relationships and associations, your values and creeds, as well as how you make money. Many people change their attitudes, ideals, ethics, public image, dress code, and philosophies. It is a good time to get out of contracts that are not good for you or to file for a divorce. It is a time when people are more blunt, combative, and lack diplomacy. You will also see a great deal of awkwardness on the world stage between diplomats and countries.

Saturn, Planet of Karma in Capricorn

From December 20, 2017 until March 22, 2020, Saturn, the planet of karma and harsh lessons, travels through Capricorn. This is great news to Sagittarius folks who, for two and a half years, felt the oppression of Saturn. Sagittarians will be free to return to their old optimistic, fun-loving selves. Saturn in Kabbalah is associated with the Sphere *Binah*, "Understanding", and wherever Saturn travels, it teaches us what we have to learn and understand. Kabbalah suggests that Saturn is the rectifier, *Tikkun*, the celestial contractor that helps fix the sign or house where it is located. It is the planet that helps us grow through crisis.

Usually Saturn transit in a sign makes it harder for people born in that sign, but since Capricorn is ruled by Saturn, it is good news for Capricorns. Saturn is their king coming back to his palace. Since Saturn enjoys traveling in Capricorn, we will all benefit from this transit as long as we are focused, disciplined, and serious. Saturn in Capricorn can help with our ambition, focus, and career. It tends to be conservative and somewhat cautious and might bring out some collective fears. Unfortunately, the dark side of Saturn in Capricorn, the conservative sign, is the rise of the alternative right on the political spectrum as well as racism and nationalism.

Capricorn is not an easy sign. In fact, in the Tarot cards, Capricorn is depicted by the card, the Devil. In late 2008, when Pluto moved into Capricorn, we experienced the Great Recession. Now that Saturn is moving into Capricorn, there is once again the danger of a bubble bursting and some economic upset, especially around May when Uranus moves into Taurus, the sign of finance. So be careful with investments from May until August.

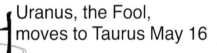

Uranus, the Fool, moves to Taurus May 16

Uranus is chaos and disorder. Uranus represents unpredictable and revolutionary behavior. Since 2010, Uranus has been in Aries, the sign of leaders and wars, and in May 2018, it is moving into Taurus. While it was in Aries, we experienced the Arab Spring, the rise and (hopefully) fall of ISIS, as well as the attempts of Putin to become Stalin. We witnessed the rise of nationalism, alternative right, alternative "truth", and a host of politicians that can be described better as jokers and fools (the Tarot card of Uranus is the Fool) rather than leaders. Since Taurus us the sign of finance, Uranus moving into that sign can create a revolution in the world economy, maybe giving a push to Bitcoin (Uranus is also technology and innovation) or an alternative financial system.

Uranus in Taurus can also instigate big discoveries and breakthroughs in science, medicine, and computing as well as the rise of an Artificial Intelligence-based economy. Of course, these trends can cause a great deal of upsets and revolutions as well as protests from people who will lose their jobs to robots. This process will continue even after April 2026 when Uranus moves to Gemini, the binary sign. During that decade (2026-2037), we can expect machines to process information as fast as humans.

From November 7, 2018 until March 5, 2019, Uranus will make a short revisit to Aries when it goes retrograde, but the year is mostly colored by Uranus in Taurus.

On a personal level, you need to rethink your finances and look into upgrading and innovating your talents. It is a time to expect some changes in your income and maybe take a leap of faith into a new field or a new source of revenue.

Chiron, the Wounded Healer Moves into Aries from April 17

On April 17, old Chiron, the wise centaur, moves into Aries. Chiron will be in Aries until April 15, 2027. In the last decade or so, he was in Pisces, the sign of religion, and he showed us clearly the danger and wounds that can come from religious fanaticism. Now Chiron, who was the teacher of all the great warriors (Hercules, Achilles, etc.), is moving into Aries, the sign of war. Chiron represents what is damaged, broken and need of healing. It is associated with wounds and shamanism. When it is in Aries, he can bring about a need to be first at everything, competitiveness to the point of injuring ourselves and others.

Be careful not to overextend yourself or fall into insecurities that can lead to overcompensation. It is good to show your vulnerability. Chiron in Aries can bring about a new class of leaders that finds strength in wisdom, sensitivity, and compassion. Chiron in Aries can also bring about new healing modalities and pioneering fields of medicine.

Last time Chiron was in Aries was 1968-1977. The flower revolution was at its peak. People were using drugs to discover themselves and break away from tradition. The cycle before was 1918-1927, the Roaring Twenties, the new world order after WWI, and a time when women were experiencing self-expression and liberation.

For all fire signs (Aries, Leo, and Sagittarius), Chiron in Aries is a powerful push towards both healing oneself and gaining healing abilities. The signs that might feel more wounded are

Capricorn and Cancer, as Chiron will force them out of their comfort zones and into action.

Chiron teaches us how to heal and deal with our mental, emotional, physical, and spiritual wounds. When it is an Aries, it favors healing methods that are associated with Aries. This means that for the next decade we have to focus on healing through action, movement, cardio, and going boldly where no one has gone before. It is the sign of pioneers. Therefore, experimental and holistic therapies can be more successful in dealing with our wounds.

Be your Own Astrologer

Here are two tips to understand how to work with the cycles of astrology. And yes, you can do it yourself:

Look into Jupiter's transits. Go back 12, 24, 36, 48, 60 years. Jupiter takes 12 years to orbit the sun and your chart. If you want to see in which aspects of life you will experience luck and flow or how prosperity would manifest in 2018, go back to 2006, 1994, 1982, etc. Wherever you experienced expansion in your life, it will return.

Examine Saturn's cycles. Saturn takes 29/30 years to orbit the sun and your chart. That is why the ages of 29-30, 58-60 are so important and are dubbed "Saturn Return". These were (or will be) the years you experience the most amount of change, consolidation, frustration, and growth. I have noticed, in the last few years, that many of the terrorists that were successful in their acts of terror were in their Saturn Return. If you want to understand the karmic lessons you are to learn this year, go back to 1988/1989. Whatever challenges, lessons, commitments, and responsibilities you experienced then, you might have to face again or benefit from the knowledge you gained in those years.

2018 Affirmation:

Thank you for leading me on my true and authentic career path so that I can prosper as well as contribute to humanity through my vocation. I am opening myself to intimacy with fellow sentient beings, asking for healing as well as the powers to heal others. I welcome synchronicities, magic, and oneness to improve my life as well as others.

Now let's go...

In some of the sections I refer to the element of your sign. You will see that I would call an Aries, a fire sign, a Fire-Bender, or a Pisces, a water sign, a Water-Bender. This is a homage to the wonderful animated Nickelodeon TV series (2005) "Avatar – The Last Air Bender". If you have a kid or an active inner child, watch this wonderful series that helps balance the elements in an entertaining way. Aries, Leo, Sagittarius are Fire-Benders; Gemini, Libra, Aquarius are Air-Benders; Cancer, Scorpio, Pisces are Water-Benders; Capricorn, Taurus, Virgo are Earth- Benders.

2018 is a year when we can grow through crisis, especially if we allow a partner-, a brother-, or a sister-in-arms to be by our side.

As you already can see, 2018 is a year designed to teach us how to become masters. It is the kind of training Yoda would give a Jedi: do or do not, no place for trying. Below you will find a detailed overview for each sign. In the sections of the signs you will read something like: Jupiter is in your house of career or Venus enters your house of health. In astrological charts there are 12 houses that symbolize areas in our lives like career, health, relationships etc. You don't have to worry about what it all means but I added the name of the houses for you to have more clarity and maybe spark an interest in studying this ancient art.

part two

The Zodiac Signs in 2018

21ᵀᴴ MARCH – 19ᵀᴴ APRIL

ARIES

Shine on You Crazy Diamond*

key phrase
I AM

element
Cardinal fire

planet
Mars

day
Tuesday

incentive
The spark

body parts
Head, blood, face, genitalia, muscles

color
Red

stone
Diamond

---

* Pink Floyd, 1975.

ARIES

The main focus in 2018 is your career and your status in your community. As the ram, the leader of the zodiac, this is super important. After all, you are the shepherded and this year you are going to shepherds' school. Saturn, the planet of karma and lessons, moved on December 20, 2017 from your house of travel and education into your house of career. The first few months of 2018, you might feel a shake-up in your career or with authority figures. It can also manifest as some concerns or issues with your father and/or father figures. But overall, since Saturn feels great in Capricorn, the sign it rules, there is a chance that through hard work you could see your career improving with a great deal of recognition and awards.

Patience, focus, discipline, and persistence can help you gain favor with Saturn in the next few years. If you are not satisfied with your chosen profession, this year you can change your career. If you are fulfilled in your path, then 2018 can bring success and well-earned recognition. Remember, your job is to lead, initiate and boldly go where no one has

ARIES ♈

gone before. You are the pioneer and this year you are asked to explore new territories in your career. If you have a plan and feel ready, this year you can transition into self-employment or a managerial position. Saturn might put you into some kind of tests or trials in your career. Like the Buddha and Jesus' three temptations, you will have to stay your course, be authentic and hold strong to your convictions. Any shortcuts in your career will be ill-fated.

 After Saturn's strict, stark, and serious nature, Jupiter comes with a breath of fresh air. Last year, Saturn was helping you understand relationships and making you more attractive, but since mid-October 2017, Jupiter moved into your house of sexuality. You can expect some sexy time! You will also experience much more intimacy and better luck with investments, productions, and working with other people's money and talents. There can be inheritance coming your way, not only from the death of a relative, but also due to sudden changes in someone's life. For example, a person gets fired and you inherit his or her job, or someone leaves town and you get to lease that person's loft. Jupiter this year will make you a shaman, a healer, and a therapist. You will see a great deal of people asking for your support and counsel. Take it seriously, since Jupiter is now in your house of magic and you are apprenticing in becoming a witch or a warlock.

From the second week of November, Jupiter, the benevolent planet and giver of gifts, will move into your house of travel and education for 12 months. That means you will experience a great deal of connection to foreigners and travel

 ARIES

abroad as well as this being a good time for teaching and learning.

This year will be initiated in the occult especially since Chiron, for the first time in 50 years, is moving into your sign. Like many Greek heroes (Achilles, Ajax, Jason, Perseus, Heracles, to name a few), you too will be initiated into the mystery of healing, martial-arts and teaching. Go find your wand!

The 5 Eclipses –
Your Emotional Landscape

Eclipses quicken processes and push events towards completion. 2018 is a year that will make you feel life is moving faster. You can expect more synchronicities and accelerated stories woven around you.

The eclipses this year are mostly in fire and air signs, which will ignite your fire and make you drive, think, text, and talk fast. You are a Fire-Bender and your flames will rise this year so please pace yourself.

The first of the eclipses, January 31, is a lunar eclipse and it pits your houses of love and children against the house of corporations and friends. You might feel pushed and pulled between the need to spend time with your children, baby projects, recreation activities, and your friends or your duty to

ARIES ♈

your company. It is best to balance both and not to make choices. It could also mean that a friend transforms into a romantic love.

 The eclipse on February 15, is a solar eclipse and falls in your house of friends and organizations. Since it is the Chinese New Year, it could mean that the next year is colored by the need to connect to community, make new friends, and open to nonprofits and altruistic organizations. It is a good time to meet new people and join clubs. It could also lead to a promotion if you work in a corporation.

 The solar eclipse on July 13 takes place in Cancer, which is not an easy sign for you. This eclipse activates your home and family, and it might make you feel vulnerable and insecure. Try to spend time with your mother or family members or maybe do a project at home (renovation, redesign).

 The lunar eclipse on July 27 is pitting friends versus romance once again, or work versus your children, or your happiness versus your company or corporation. You could feel torn and pushed in different directions. However, since it is the biblical day of love and it is activating your house of love, it could bring a new love into your life. Maybe a new person or maybe a new hobby.

 The solar eclipse on August 11 falls in your house of love and sports once again. It is a good time to embark on a new hobby or start a new physical activity.

♈ ARIES

Mercury Retrograde – Mental Landscape

During Mercury retrograde it is not recommended to start new long-term projects, sign documents, make large purchases, get married, publish, start marketing campaigns, or release new products. Communications of all sorts are slower and filled with glitches and challenges. Computers crash, stock markets turn volatile, flights are delayed, traffic is worse than usual, accidents occur more often, and Murphy's Law takes hold of our lives. For example, the infamous Flash Crash of May 6, 2010, took place during Mercury retrograde in Taurus (the sign of money and the stock market).

If you must start a new project, be as mindful as you can. Pay attention to small details and read in between the lines if you must sign a document. Rewrite your emails, edit your texts and think before you speak. In fact, it is better if you spend more time listening than talking. Life does not come to a halt during Mercury retrograde. You can still achieve a great deal. Mercury retro is like going on a vacation while it is raining. It is still possible but not much fun. However, it is a great time to edit, redo, reexamine yourself and your path, revisit old projects, and find lost objects. It is said that there are more coincidences and more synchronicities when Mercury is retrograding. Try to focus on activities that have the prefix *re* – reevaluate, reedit, redo, reexamine, reconnect, regenerate, revisit, re-imagine etc.

ARIES

This year Mercury is retrograding in fire signs. Because you belong to the fire clan, it might be a bit easier compared to other years. As a Fire-Bender, you might experience some magical moments during the retrogrades.

Between March 22 and April 15, Mercury is retrograding in Aries, your tribe. This is the most intense Mercury retrograde for you this year. Watch where you are going, how you drive, and how you dress and present yourself. There might be some illness or injuries. Please boost your immune system. However, the retrograde can also help reconnect you to parts of your personality you thought you lost (passion, enthusiasm) that can lead to a new self-expression.

Between July 26 and August 18, Mercury is retrograding in Leo. If you have children, they can drive you crazy around this time. So be patient. Past loves might resurrect. Be careful of sports injuries. You might find yourself more entertaining and funny during this time.

Between November 16 and December 6, Mercury is retrograding in Sagittarius and Scorpio. Be extra careful when traveling or if you are abroad. Double check flights, visas, local customs, etc. Maybe some issues with in-laws or teachers.

♈ ARIES

Unpredictable Finances

From 2010, Uranus moved into your sign making life feel like a roller-coaster. It happens every 84 years, therefore, from May 2018, you will no longer need to host Uranus and deal with his unpredictability and capriciousness. Since 2010 a great deal of change and revolution happened in your life and now you can expect a bit more stability.

In May 2018, Uranus moves into Taurus and will stay there until 2026. Uranus will be transiting into your house of finance, talents and self-worth. This means that you really have to watch your financial situation from May. Uranus is called "the Joker" or "the Fool". It is chaotic but also ingenious. You might suddenly get an "aha" moment that can actually help your finances and give you an original idea or a bright inkling about your earning potential. Even if you cannot manifest the idea right now, write it down. In the future, it can come to life.

Uranus might inspire you to take a jump and a leap of faith into something totally new regarding your talents and finances. Maybe a new field of study that can later translate into a new revenue stream. Uranus favors technology, innovation, and science. Maybe you can think of a great new application or an e-commerce business. It is also a good time to redo your web site, give your Facebook page a face lift, and connect to social media.

ARIES ♈

Mars – Your Leader Retrograding

Mars is your ruler, and therefore channels itself through your actions and behavior. Mars is your guide as well as personal trainer. Mars is the planet of action, passion, and movement. It is your nuclear reactor. It is your solar panel and battery. It is also the planet ruling seeds and vegetation. Since not all of us are farmers, it translates to whatever projects, creation, and enterprises we plan and sow in our lives.

When Mars is retrograding (June 26 to August 27), the aspects it governs don't work so well. Metaphorically speaking, the fields we tend don't yield good crops. That does not mean nothing will happen. Sometimes it is actually good to walk backwards. Think of the reverse gear in your car. Where would you be without it? How would you ever be able to park or adjust your position?

As is the rule with all retrograde planets, during the retro period it is safe to engage in any activity that has the prefix re – redo, revert, reject etc. During Mars Retrograde, you can revisit old projects, make peace, reconnect to past brothers- and sisters-in-arms, reexamine your sexuality and passion, as well as undergo a great deal of healing. However, it is not recommended to buy big machinery (cars, appliances) or start a war or a lawsuit (whoever shoots first loses). It is not a good time to start a sexual relationship or launch a big project. Not the best for surgery (unless absolutely needed). Try not to be reactive or overly self-protective, especially during

 ARIES

Mercury Retro that overlaps Mars Retro between July 26 and August 18.

Since you are ruled by Mars, during July and August, it will be harder for you to see the path you are walking, and it can create unnecessary wars, aggression, arguments, impulsiveness, and strife in your life. Stay calm. Spend time in water (to cool off). And exercise patience. Mars will be retrograding in your house of community, friends, government, and companies between June 26 until August 13. There might be some conflict within your company, change of leadership, or reshuffling around you that can affect your position. A friend might be going through some hardship and need your help. From August 13 to 27, Mars will be exalted and retrograding in Capricorn in your house of career. Mars can cause some struggles with bosses or authority figures. It might make it

harder for you to lead or people will undermine your authority.

In September, your life will change for the better and you can expect some good news or promotion in your career. Projects that were held up will be released, and your energy level, passion and mojo will return.

ARIES ♈

Venus: Money and Love

Venus is the ruler of comfort, luxury, finance, talents, values, art, and relationships. She is also associated with Maat, the goddess of justice and law. Venus works in beauty cycles: the more you love yourself, the more you believe in yourself. The better your self-image, the more you connect to your talents. The more you develop and invest in your talent, the more money you can make. Venus' message is: love yourself and money will follow. Some, however, think that the more money they make, the more they would love themselves, and that is a mistake.

This year, Venus will retrograde between October 6 and November 16. First Venus retrogrades in Scorpio and then, from October 31, she will retrograde in Libra. When Venus is retrograding in Scorpio, she can affect your finance, investments, and your passion. In general, avoid forming any partnerships and, if possible, don't make big investments or purchases. For you as an Aries, Venus retrograding in Scorpio can undo relationships, cause breakups, and make you say things you regret. When Venus retrogrades in Libra, it can create challenges but also profound lessons in relationships and partnerships. Venus retro can also show you who are your true allies as well as your real enemies. It can also manifest as extra martial affairs, bad investments, disappointments with intimate relationships, and some negativity from people who are envious or jealous.

 ARIES

Since Venus also rules value, it is a good time to review and change your attitudes, aspirations, and values. Venus Retro is actually a great time to buy secondhand goods. It is also a good time to sell things you don't need. However, if you have secret love affairs, this is the time most of them are discovered.

This year, Venus will be in your sign between March 6 and 31, making your more attractive, helping you get a raise or tap into a new talent. It is a great time for romance, making money, and connecting to your artistic side. This is a good time for you to rebrand yourself, dress differently, change your hair, get some new clothes. Not a bad time to indulge and pamper yourself (as long as it is healthy and does not harm you or anyone else).

Conclusion:

This year there is change in your career and an opportunity to discover your true passion and calling. Watch July and August, when Mars is retrograding, not to be over-demanding and aggressive or burned out. Love can come your way, but it can be short-lived and explosive if you make choices based on old patters and behaviors. And be nice to your bosses. They can make you or break you this year. Since Chiron is moving to your sign this year, a once-in-a-50-year cycle, you will have to learn a new way to express yourself. Your leadership will have to change and incorporate more tenderness, therapy, and shamanism.

20ᵀᴴ APRIL – 20ᵀᴴ MAY

TAURUS ♉

*Don't you know the joker laughs
at you?**

key phrase
I HAVE

element
Fixed (unchangeable) earth

planet
Venus

day
Friday

incentive
Supporter

body parts
Throat, neck, thyroid gland

color
Red-orange

stone
Jade

---

* The Beatles, 1967.

♉ TAURUS

 In the last few years, Saturn, the planet of karma and harsh lessons, was in your house of death and sexuality. It was not easy, since Saturn forcefully demanded you to change, morph, peel, and shed your old skin. Saturn forced a great deal of changes in all aspects of your life. But 2018 is the year you can emerge out of the cocoon, spread your wings, and become a butterfly. Yes, you are a phoenix rising out of the ashes of your former self. In 2018, Saturn connects you to a foreign culture or to people or philosophies coming from abroad. Saturn can also propel you to embark on a new study. Teaching what you want to learn and learning what you want to teach will be your mantra for the next few years.

I highly recommend studying a new language. Whenever you learn a new language, the skills you possessed when you spoke that language in past lives return to you. It as if the language is stored in the same place these abilities hide and opening your mind to one leads to the other. Since your sign is the sign of talents, you can expect a new language to lead to new talents. These talents can later translate into financial gains.

Saturn is moving into your house of truth and therefore will demand authenticity. Now that you are finished peeling and shedding, you have a chance to decide who you are and what you believe in. Remember what Lao Tzu, the great Taoist, once said: "there is your truth, my truth, and the Truth". Your job will be to discern between these three so called "truths".

From mid-May, Uranus will move into your sign for the first time in 84 years. People born in the beginning of Taurus

TAURUS ♉

(April 20-23) will experience a great deal of change in their lives as Uranus transits over their sun. It is as if they are on a roller-coaster. Enjoy the ride and welcome change with open hands especially from May until August.

 With Saturn's strict, stark, and serious nature, Jupiter comes with some good news. Last year, Jupiter was helping you understand your work and how to serve others. In 2017, you might have received a promotion, clarity about your work or diet, as well as how to better serve humanity. Maybe even a new pet? But since mid-October, 2017, Jupiter moved into Scorpio, your opposite sign. This year you can expect good news in regards to relationships, marriage, and partnerships in your private life and work. If you have any lawsuits or enemies that stand in your path, Jupiter will be like the great Ganesh, the elephant headed god who removes obstacles. You will have luck, power, and resources to deal with your antagonists this year.

Since Jupiter is transiting in your opposite sign, be careful of over-extending yourself, overstretching, and over-training, since Jupiter is opposite to your sign and you might get "full of yourself" or over-confident.

From the second week of November, Jupiter, the benevolent planet and giver of gifts, will move into your house of inheritance, sexuality, and partner's money for 12 months. That will help you connect to your passion and, if you have a partner, afford him or her the ability to make more money.

 TAURUS

The 5 Eclipses – Your Emotional Landscape

As I mentioned earlier, eclipses quicken processes and push events towards completion. 2018 is a year that will make you feel that life is moving faster. You can expect more synchronicities and accelerated stories woven around you.

The eclipses this year are on the Leo/Aquarius axis. Both of these signs are not easy for you to handle or channel, since they are fixed signs just like you. And fixed signs are stubborn. They don't like to bend, move, or change. In fact, in Kabbalah, Taurus, Leo, Aquarius, and Scorpio are considered to be the four creatures named "Hayot", who hold the Throne of God. Please be extra cautious this year during the eclipses. Don't overload your schedule around the eclipses and try to chill out.

The lunar eclipse on January 31 can be especially emotional and challenging for your career, as well as for home, family, motherhood, real-estate, and a general feeling of insecurity. However, this crisis can lead to a great deal of growth. While life might become intense in January/February, it can also push you into action and unclog obstacles in your life. You might experience a push and pull between home and career. Try to balance both.

TAURUS ♉

The solar eclipse on February 15 is focused on your career as well as on father figures. You can expect some revelation or a new discovery in your professional life. Things will move faster in your work.

The solar eclipse on July 13 is far easier and smoother as it is in Cancer, a water sign that is easy for you to flow with. If you are a garden, cancer is your fountain and sprinkle system. There could be some news regarding a sibling, a business opportunity, and contracts. Communication and networking with flow. It is a good time to write.

The lunar eclipse on July 27, which is the biblical day of love, pits home against family, and you might feel pulled in both directions, unable to satisfy either. Remember that free will is on your side. So do something every day for your home or family and something for your career. Your parents at that time might be demanding.

The solar eclipse on August 11 is focused on home. So take time to relax and nest. Even though it is Mercury retrograde, it is a good time to contemplate or plan a move (not buy a place but plan and research). The eclipse can also help remove an obstacle around your familial relationship and resolve conflict at home.

Mercury Retrograde – Mental Landscape

During Mercury retrograde, it is not recommended to start new long-term projects, sign documents, make large purchases, get married, publish, start marketing campaigns, or release new products. It is not easy for you, I know. Your sign's key words are "I Have", and this prohibition against making purchases and using shopping as therapy can be tough. But you can keep it safe by donating an object whenever you do end up buying something.

Communications of all sorts are slower and filled with glitches and challenges. Computers crash, stock markets turn volatile, flights are delayed, traffic is worse than usual, accidents occur more often, and Murphy's Law takes hold of our lives. For example, the infamous Flash Crash of May 6, 2010, took place while Mercury was retrograde in your sign. As you know from the raging bull statue on Wall Street, Taurus is the sign of money and stock markets. Be careful of any similar Flash Crash in your own life.

If you must start a new project, be as mindful as you can. Pay attention to small details and read in between the lines if you must sign a document. Rewrite your emails, edit your texts, and think before you speak. In fact, it is better if you spend more time listening than talking.

Life does not come to a halt during Mercury retrograde. You can still achieve a great deal. Mercury retro is like going on a vacation while it is raining. It is still possible but not much fun. However, it is a great time to edit, redo, reexamine yourself

and your path, revisit old projects, and find lost objects. It is said that there are more coincidences and more synchronicities when Mercury is retrograding. Try to focus on activities that have the prefix *re* – reevaluate, reedit, redo, reexamine, reconnect, regenerate, revisit, re-imagine, etc.

This year, Mercury is retrograding in fire signs. You might feel a bit of a push or a kick in the butt. You are an Earth Bender and fire doesn't mix very well with soil. For this reason, take your time and be extra patient this year during the retrogrades.

 From March 22 to April 15, Mercury is retrograding in Aries. Sometimes you can be a stubborn bull, and with Mercury in Aries, the Aries cowboy comes to push you to better pastures. This Mercury retrograde is in your house of letting go, past lifetimes, hidden enemies, and confinement. Choose your words wisely, since you can easily make enemies through your writing, texts, posts, calls, or emails. However, people from past lives or from your past in this life can make a comeback. Also, a great deal of dreams and synchronicities can give you a new sense of direction. It is a great time for meditations and insights from the upper worlds.

 From July 26 to August 18, Mercury is retrograding in Leo, which is not comfortable for you. Leo is another stubborn sign and fire and can be too egocentric for you. This can manifest as misunderstanding at home or with family members. There can be issues around ego and a lot of drama around you that push you into action you might not want to take. Not a good time to buy properties.

♉ TAURUS

From November 16 to December 6, Mercury is retrograding in Sagittarius and Scorpio. Be extra careful with investments and with marriage or business partners. This retrograde can cause a great deal of havoc with significant others, lawsuits, and enemies.

Unpredictable Journey

As I mentioned in the intro, in 2010, Uranus, the planet of chaos, unpredictability, and revolutions, moved into Aries. It was transiting since then in your house of letting go, causing you sudden separations from people, possessions, and attitudes. Not all was bad. As a fixed sign, you need to be reminded that you don't need all that you have and that what you want is not always what you need. You also opened up to mysticism and to your intuition. Maybe you even met some people you might have known in previous lives.

On May 16, 2018, Uranus moves into your sign, the sign of finance, money, talent, and self-worth. We can expect an unpredictable May, June, and July, especially in the finance world, as whenever Uranus moves into a sign, the first few months are somewhat chaotic.

Uranus comes into your sign once every 84 years, a rare and infrequent cycle. It means that, for the next decade, you will experience some unpredictability. It can be frightening but also exciting. It is not bad. It is freaky but not bad. It is scary but

TAURUS ♉

not bad. It is time for change and embracing the new. As a fixed earth sign, change is not your strength, but you need a shakeup and it is coming. Even the trees need to be shaken to let their fruits fall. However, since it is happening in your first house, the house of self, body, and personality, it might affect your health and change your self-expression. It can also be good for you. For example, you will connect to your humor and become funnier, laugh more often (sometimes at yourself), and become more charismatic. You might try new things, dress differently, and get crazy ingenious ideas. But, it can also make you a rebel without a cause and make you feel like you want to break away from everything, even from good things. Be careful not to be enslaved to freedom. Even an air balloon needs sandbags.

Mars Retrograde

Mars is the planet of action, passion, and movement. It is your nuclear reactor. It is your solar panel and battery. It is also the planet ruling seeds and vegetation, which is so important to Taurus, the Mother Nature sign. Since not all of us are farmers, it translates to whatever projects, creations, and enterprises we plan and sow in our lives. When Mars is retrograding (June 26 to August 27), these aspects of life don't work so well. Metaphorically speaking, these fields we tend don't yield good crops. That does not mean nothing will happen. Sometimes it is actually good to walk backwards. Think of the reverse gear in your car. Where would

TAURUS

you be without it? How would you ever be able to park or adjust your position?

During Mars retrograde, you can revisit old projects, make peace, reconnect to past brothers- and sisters-in-arms, reexamine your sexuality and passion, as well as undergo a great deal of healing. As is the rule with all retrograde planets, during the retro period it is safe to engage in any activity that has the prefix re – redo, revert, reject, etc. However, it is not recommended to buy big machinery (cars, appliances) or start a war or a lawsuit (whoever shoots first loses). It is not a good time to start a sexual relationship or launch a big project. Not the best for surgery (unless absolutely needed). Try not to be reactive or overly self-protective, especially during Mercury retro that overlaps Mars retro between July 26 and August 18.

When Mars retrogrades in Aquarius June 26 until August 13, you might experience conflict in career or with authority figures. Some of your projects can bring frustration or your actions in your professional life might be misinterpreted. Mars retrograde in Capricorn August 13 to August 27: strife while traveling or with in-laws, teachers, and educators.

In September, once Mars goes direct, a great deal of projects that were held back can start flowing better. It is far more recommended to travel abroad after August 28. Since Mars will be in Capricorn, a fellow Earth Bender, you will feel a big surge of energy and power. Your career and work will flow better from September onward.

TAURUS ♉

Venus: Money and Love

Venus is your ruler and therefore all of her cycles are far more influential for you. Venus is the ruler of comfort, luxury, finance, talents, values, art, and relationships. She is also associated with Maat, the goddess of justice and law. When Venus is in your sign, you feel attractive, and you get compliments. That, in turn, raises your self-esteem and how you value yourself, which can contribute to your ability to make money or believe in your talents.

Venus works in beauty cycles: the more you love yourself, the more you believe in yourself. The better your self-image, the more you connect to your talents. The more you develop and invest in your talent, the more money you can make. Venus' message is: love yourself and money will follow. Some, however, think that the more money they make, the more they would love themselves, and that is a mistake. This year during Venus retrograde (October 6 – November 16), you will be able to change your attitude and fix your relationship to money.

This year, Venus will retrograde between October 6 to November 16. First Venus retrogrades in Scorpio (October 6-31) and then it will retrograde in Libra (October 31 – Nov 16). When it is retrograding in Scorpio, it can affect your finance, your investments, and your passion. In general, avoid forming any partnerships and if possible don't make big investments or purchases. Venus is retrograding in your house of relationships. Therefore, all your contractual relationships

Ⴆ TAURUS

will go through scrutiny. When Venus retrogrades in Libra, she can create challenges but also profound lessons in your workspace, in your health, or in relationships with employees or people who help or serve you. Since Venus also rules value, it is a good time to review and change your attitudes, aspirations, and values. Venus retro is actually a great time to buy second hand goods. It is also a good time to sell things you don't need. However, if you have secret love affairs, this is the time most of them are discovered.

As you already know, Venus is your queen and the ruler of your sign. You feel its aspects much more than other signs. Venus is in your sign between March 31 to April 24 making you far more attractive to others. It is a great time for romance, making money, and connecting to your artistic side. This is a good time for you to rebrand yourself, dress differently, change your hair, get some new clothes. Not a bad time to indulge and pamper yourself (as long as it is healthy and does not harm you or anyone else).

Conclusion:

You are free from a long period of stagnation and death and it is a time to be more authentic and real. Some unpredictability is coming your way from May onward but it is a welcome change. With both Venus and Jupiter activating your house of relationships, it is a good year to collaborate, bring partners into your life, and work on your relationships. It is an exciting year. So go find someone to share the adventures with!

21TH MAY – 20TH JUNE

GEMINI ♊

Let it be, let it be, speaking words of wisdom, let it be*

Key phrase
I THINK

Element
Mutable (changeable) air

Planet
Mercury, the messenger of gods

Day
Wednesday

Incentive
Flexibility

Body parts
Arms, lungs, nervous system

Color
Orange

Stone
Rock crystal

---

* The Beatles, 1970.

♊ GEMINI

In the last few years, Saturn has been forcing you to reassess your significant relationships. Saturn, known in Kabbalah as the rectifier, has been instigating situations in marriage and partners in work to teach you the value of significant others. You felt like your partners provoked you and pushed your buttons, trying to get you to lose your cool. This is all changing in 2018. Saturn is now shifting into your house of death and transformation. In the next few years, Saturn will teach you lessons around passion and sexuality. He will allow you to see what you are attracting into your life, what motivates and drives you, and how good you are at saying "goodbye". Your priorities will change and you will gain more clarity about what is important in life. No more superficiality, this year you are deep diving into your true nature. Since Saturn is visiting your house of death, you will have to learn the lesson of letting go and releasing. There are dead things in your life that need to be buried. You need to practice shedding. Just be careful not to throw the baby out with the bathwater.

This year, your partner might change the way he or she makes money or might experience some financial difficulties, but if you play your cards right, you might be able to produce, connect, and manage other people's talents and money. It is a

GEMINI ♊

time for you to believe and connect to your true power. The house of death is also the house of magic and the occult. Intuition, powerful insights, and the ability to generate intimacy will be a major part of your life and work. You might meet people from past lives and connect to skills you had in previous lives. Just let go and things will come your way.

 With Saturn's strict, stark, and serious nature, Jupiter brings some good news. Last year, Jupiter was helping you in love, with children, and with your creativity. But since mid-October 2017, you started receiving good news relating to work and health. It is a good time to expand your work, hire employees, and find a way to serve humanity. You might get a promotion and receive more responsibilities that you will be able to carry with no trouble at all. You will find your schedule being overbooked. So be careful not to say "yes" to too many projects or assignments. Pace yourself! It is a good year to embark on a new diet and health routine. If you were looking for a time to heal physically and mentally, 2018 can be your year. In addition, especially as it is the Year of the Dog and Jupiter is in your house of pets, consider getting a dog, cat, parrot.

From the second week of November, Jupiter, the benevolent planet and giver of gifts, will move into your house of relationships for 12 months. This is the best time to get married, win lawsuits, and find a business partner.

Ⅱ GEMINI

The 5 Eclipses –
Your Emotional Landscape

As I mentioned in the introduction, eclipses quicken processes and push events towards completion. 2018 is a year that will make you feel life is moving faster. You can expect more synchronicities and accelerated stories woven around you.

The eclipses this year fall on the Leo/Aquarius axis. These signs are easy for you to work with, as you are an Air Bender and the fire/air eclipses will feel familiar.

During the lunar eclipse of Jan 31, you will make a great deal of connections with people from your country as well as with foreigners. It is a good time to publish and write, push forward enterprises, and market yourself. But eclipses are eclipses and werewolves have claws. Be careful nevertheless and don't get cocky.

The solar eclipse on February 15, is focused in the house of in-laws, truth, education, and travel. Some issues with your in-laws might come to light but also processes that have to do with teaching, learning, and travel will manifest with the eclipse. Since it is happening in the Chinese New Year, it might mean travel and education will be the focus of the year.

GEMINI Ⅱ

The solar eclipse on July 13 is more emotional as it is happening in Cancer and takes place in your house of finance. This water eclipse is not easy for you. Be extra careful with your spending and investments.

 The lunar eclipse on July 27 pushes and pulls you, forcing your dual nature to come across more strongly. It will be focused especially around your connections and people you do business with. It will tempt you to lie or bend the truth. Be strong and don't compromise your authentic core. It can also cause problems with siblings and relatives.

 The solar eclipse of August 11 is in your house of communication and, since it is in Leo, it can actually be entertaining and interesting. It is during Mercury retro. So please pay extra attention to what you say, text, post, and write. Your communications might come across as roaring or too dramatic, especially since it is happening during Mercury retrograde.

 ## Mercury Retrograde – Mental Landscape

Mercury is your planet and every year, while Mercury is retrograding, you experience the cosmic mental breakdown more severely than other signs. We depend on you, Gemini, to deliver our messages and translate life to us but, when your planet is on strike, you feel helpless and we all suffer. Remember, during Mercury retrograde, it is not

 GEMINI

recommended to start new long-term projects, sign documents, make large purchases, get married, publish, start marketing campaigns, or release new products. Communications of all sorts are slower and filled with glitches and challenges. Computers crash, stock markets turn volatile, flights are delayed, traffic is worse than usual, accidents occur more often, and Murphy's Law takes hold of our lives. For example, the infamous Flash Crash of May 6, 2010 took place during Mercury Retrograde in Taurus (the sign of money and the stock market).

If you must start a new project, be as mindful as you can. Pay attention to small details and read in between the lines if you must sign a document. Rewrite your emails, edit your texts, and think before you speak. In fact, it is better if you spend more time listening than talking. Life does not come to a halt during Mercury retrograde. You can still achieve a great deal.

Mercury retro is like going on a vacation while it is raining. It is still possible but not much fun. However, it is a great time to edit, redo, reexamine yourself and your path, revisit old projects, and find lost objects. It is said that there are more coincidences and more synchronicities when Mercury is retrograding. Try to focus on activities that have the prefix *re* – reevaluate,

GEMINI Ⅱ

reedit, redo, reexamine, reconnect, regenerate, revisit, re-imagine, etc.

This year, Mercury is retrograding in fire signs, which is actually good for you, since you are an Air Bender and fire feeds you with passion and motivation.

 The first retrograde this year is between March 22 to April 15. This Mercury retrograde is in Aries and is activating your house of community and friends. You will experience more chaos with some colleagues or people in your company, club, or organization. Maybe some issues with government bureaucracy. However, it is a good time to reconnect with friends you have not seen in a long time and ask forgiveness.

 Between July 26 and August 18, Mercury retrogrades in Leo. This can manifest as misunderstandings with siblings, roommates, and neighbors as well as issues with contracts. Definitely try to avoid signing documents this retro and do not start new businesses. For you, this retro is a double retro. And since the eclipse also takes place during this time, be extra cautious.

 Between November 16 and December 6, Mercury retrogrades in Sagittarius and Scorpio. This is your opposite sign. So you might have some issues with your partners and relationships. Difficulties with lawsuits and enemies. A good time to come out of contracts you do not need anymore or file for divorce. The last week of the retro is in your house of health. So take extra care with your diet, work, and routine.

♊ GEMINI

Unpredictable Journey

In 2010, Uranus, the planet of chaos, unpredictability, and revolutions, moved into Aries. For the last 7 years, Uranus was in your house of friends and companies. There were a lot of disruption and changes within your circle of friends and/or organizations. Some people stormed in and out of your life, leaving you feeling a bit confused. There also might have been unexpected issues with government, taxes, and permits.

On May 16, 2018, Uranus moves into Taurus, your next-door neighbor, and will stay there for almost a decade. It is not comfortable. It is as if someone is building a nuclear plant down your street. Uranus will now transit through your house of past lives and confinement. You might find yourself trapped or secluded, dealing with a feeling of abandonment. Remember, it is only a feeling. It does not mean that it is really happening. Uranus teaches the lesson of impermanence. Even if it is tough, it can change overnight. The more you release, surrender, and let go, the more positive flow and success will come your way. With Saturn in your house of death and Uranus in your house of surrender, you can let go of whatever you don't like about yourself. It can be extra weight, bad career choices, evil bosses, blocks in a relationship, destructive attitudes, smoking cigarettes, etc.

GEMINI ♊

Mars Retrograde

Mars is the planet of action, passion, and movement. It is your nuclear reactor. It is your solar panel and battery. It is also the planet ruling seeds and vegetation. Since not all of us are farmers, it translates to whatever projects, creation, and and enterprises we plan and sow in our lives. When Mars is retrograding (June 26 to August 27), these aspects of life don't work so well. Metaphorically speaking, these fields we tend don't yield good crops. That does not mean nothing will happen. Sometimes it is actually good to walk backwards. Think of the reverse gear in your car. Where would you be without it? How would you ever be able to park or adjust your position?

During Mars retrograde, you can revisit old projects, make peace, reconnect to past brothers- and sisters-in-arms, reexamine your sexuality and passion, as well as undergo a great deal of healing. As is the rule with all retrograde planets, during the retro period, it is safe to engage in any activity that has the prefix *re* – redo, revert, reject, etc. However, it is not recommended to buy big machinery (cars, appliances) or start a war or a lawsuit (whoever shoots first loses). It is not a good time to start a sexual relationship or launch a big project. Not the best for surgery (unless absolutely needed). Try not to be reactive or overly self-protective, especially during Mercury retro that overlaps Mars retro between July 26 and August 18.

♊ GEMINI

Mars retrogrades in Aquarius, June 26 until August 13: since Mars is retrograding in your house of truth and philosophy, make sure you don't lie! Mercury, your ruler, is the god of liars and thieves. It is a theme this year, so take heed. There is no such thing as "alternative truth". So don't be tempted. In addition, between June 26 to August 13, Mars is retro in your house of travel and foreign cultures. It can cause injuries or conflict with foreigners or while traveling.

 Mars retrogrades in Capricorn, August 13 to August 27: Mars enters your house of death. It is the peak of your process of letting go and experiencing the death that Saturn introduces. It is not good time for investments, especially since Mercury is also retrograding at the same time. You might feel that your passion and sexuality are changing and what you attract and are attracted to are also morphing.

In September, once Mars goes direct, a great deal of projects that were held back can start flowing better. It will be better to invest then and you will feel your mojo returning and your zeal for life resurrecting.

GEMINI ♊

Venus: Money and Love

Venus is the ruler of comfort, luxury, finance, talents, values, art, and relationships. She is also associated with Maat, the goddess of justice and law.

Venus works in beauty cycles: the more you love yourself, the more you believe in yourself. The better your self-image, the more you connect to your talents. The more you develop and invest in your talents, the more money you can make. Venus' message is: love yourself and money will follow. Some, however, think that the more money they make, the more they would love themselves and that is a mistake. This year during Venus retrograde (October 6 – November 16), you will be able to change your attitude and fix your relationship to money.

This year, Venus will retrograde between October 6 and November 16. First Venus retrogrades in Scorpio (October 6-31), and then it will retrograde in Libra (October 31 – Nov 16). When she is retrograding in Scorpio, it can affect your finances, investments, and your passion. In general, avoid forming any partnerships and if possible don't make

big investments or purchases. While Venus is retrograding in Scorpio, she will be in your house of work and health. Pay extra attention to your diet and your routine. She can also cause issues with employees. When Venus

♊ GEMINI

retrogrades in Libra, she can create challenges but also profound lessons in relationships and partnerships, especially with your children and lovers. Venus retro can also show you who your true allies as well as real enemies are. Since Venus also rules value, it is a good time to review and change your attitudes, aspirations, and values.

 Venus is in your sign between April 24 and May 19, making you far more attractive to others. It is a great time for romance, making money, and connecting to your artistic side. This is a good time for you to rebrand yourself, dress differently, change your hair, and get some new clothes. Not a bad time to indulge and pamper yourself (as long as it is healthy and does not harm you or anyone else).

Conclusion:

This is a year of letting go of whatever holds you back. It is a year of transformation as well as magic. While death is dancing a tango with you, it can actually be sexy and allow you to connect to your true powers. Your health and work can improve, and you will find opportunities to expand by focusing and cutting excesses.

GEMINI ♊

21TH JUNE – 22ND JULY

CANCER

Love, love me do, you know I love you*

key phrase
I FEEL

element
Cardinal water

planet
The Moon, which gives us light in the darkest hour

day
Monday

incentive
Birth

body parts
Ribs, stomach, chest, internal organs, womb

color
Orange-yellow

stone
Pearl

---

* The Beatles, 1962.

 CANCER

In the last few years, Saturn, the Lord Karma and grand teacher, has been teaching you some harsh lessons through your health and work. Many of your clan experienced hardship with diets, routine, and the ability to serve. You might have felt like your efforts were not rewarded and that no matter how much you try, you could not achieve your goals. So here is some good news: it is over! In 2018, work should flow much better and, towards the end of the year, Jupiter will enter your house of health and work and will begin the process of healing.

In the last few weeks of 2017, Saturn moved into your house of relationships and marriage. Since it is the house of all contractual relationships as well as justice and law, those are the areas of life where you will have to grow through crisis. If you are in a relationship, then this period can bring challenges with your partner or maybe your partner will go through some difficulties in his or her life. If you don't have a partner, then there is a chance, especially at the end of the year, of attracting a significant other. Saturn is not all bad. Saturn galvanizes what is already there. If there is confusion in your partnerships in life or partnerships at work, then Saturn will make them far more difficult. If you are serious about finding a partner and you can demonstrate you have overcome past patterns, for example, by saying "no" to wrong candidates, then you will find Saturn helping you get the right relationship. If you suffer from obstacles and patterns with your business partners or love relationships, then Saturn, in the next few years, can help fix them.

CANCER

In astrology, the house of partners is also the house of enemies. It is possible that you will have to confront and conquer your antagonists. After all, your enemies and your partners all serve as your mirror, and they are there to make you grow (directly or indirectly).

 With Saturn's strict, stark, and serious nature, Jupiter comes with a breath of fresh air. Last year, Jupiter was helping you get your home and family in order, and this year it is all about love. Jupiter is entering your house of love, happiness, children, and creativity. It is amazing news as we just saw that Saturn will be in your house of marriage. When we fall in love, we treat our lover like royalty, but then Saturn comes and consolidates the love into a relationship, which is when we start treating our partner like we treat ourselves. This year you will be able to have your cake and eat it. You can experience love and a relationship simultaneously. If you are married, it does not mean that you need to have an extramarital relationship. It might manifest as a rekindling of your love to your partner or a new hobby or sport that ignites your love and passion.

Jupiter will also help you have fun, which you need to badly. It can also help you connect to children and get pregnant. 2018 is a year when you can find yourself reconnecting to recreation, sports, or any other activity that brings out your inner child.

From the second week of November, Jupiter, the benevolent planet and giver of gifts, will move into your house of health and work for 12 months. Jupiter will open doors for healing and promotion in work.

 CANCER

The 5 Eclipses – Your Emotional Landscape

As we saw earlier, eclipses quicken processes and push events towards completion. 2018 is a year that will make you feel life is moving faster. You can expect more synchronicities and accelerated stories woven around you. The moon is the ruler of your sign and therefore is far more important to you. Always try to follow the cycles of the moon. On the new moon, start a project. On the full moon, rest. And when the moon is waning, edit or cut things out of your life.

The eclipses this year fall on the axis of Leo/Aquarius, and both signs are not easy for you to handle or channel. You are a Water Bender and fire (Leo) and air (Aquarius) do not mix well with your watery compassion. Take your time around the eclipses (I know some people already think you are too slow sometimes), and pace yourself and your feelings. Don't withdraw into your shell. Stay engaged. We need you!

The lunar eclipse on January 31 is causing tensions around finances, both in your income and with your partner (in life or work). The lunation also activates your house of passion, sexuality, and death. You will be asked to let go of something in your life and to look deeper into what motivates and drives you. You might get an insight to what will be your mission this year.

The solar eclipse on February 15 is focused on your house of death and transformation. There is a lot of magic in the air. You will feel more inti-

CANCER

mate and experience a surge in your sexuality. But it is also the house of death. So you will experience an intense letting go.

The solar eclipse on July 13 is far more personal as it takes place in Cancer, your sign. It can affect your body, your chosen path, your personality, and your image.

The lunar eclipse on July 27 pits your needs against your partner's. It can move things faster with finances, inheritance, taxes, and insurance.

The solar eclipse on August 11 is in your house of finance again. This could mean some change in the way you make money or a new talent being rewarded. However, eclipses are unpredictable and can create chaos in your finances. So make sure you are very aware of your spending, especially since it is happening during Mercury retrograde.

 ## Mercury Retrograde – Mental Landscape

During Mercury retrograde, it is not recommended to start new long-term projects, sign documents, make large purchases, get married, publish, start marketing campaigns, or release new products. Communications of all sorts are slower and filled with glitches and challenges. Computers crash, stock markets turn volatile, flights are delayed, traffic is worse than usual, accidents occur more often, and Murphy's

CANCER

Law takes hold of our lives. For example, the infamous Flash Crash of May 6, 2010, took place during Mercury Retrograde in Taurus (the sign of money and the stock market).

If you must start a new project, be as mindful as you can. Pay attention to small details and read in-between the lines if you must sign a document. Rewrite your emails, edit your texts, and think before you speak. In fact, it is better if you spend more time listening than talking. Life does not come to a halt during Mercury retrograde. You can still achieve a great deal. Mercury retro is like going on a vacation while it is raining. It is still possible but not much fun. However, it is a great time to edit, redo, reexamine yourself and your path, revisit old projects, and find lost objects. It is said that there are more coincidences and more synchronicities when Mercury is retrograding. Try to focus on activities that have the prefix re – reevaluate, reedit, redo, reexamine, reconnect, regenerate, revisit, re-imagine, etc.

This year, Mercury is retrograding in fire signs, which might be a bit harder for you as you are made of water. But maybe a bit of fire can ignite you to move to different fields and push you forward.

CANCER

The first Mercury retrogrades happen between March 22 and April 15. Mercury retrogrades in Aries, which is a tough sign for you. Cancer represents compassion, and Aries is the ruthless warrior. This Mercury retrograde takes place in your house of career. There could be misunderstandings and issues in communication in your professional life, at work, with your father, or with authority figures. It is a great time to revisit past projects but not to start new ones.

 From July 26 to August 18, Mercury retrogrades in Leo. This can be a bit hard on your finances and self-worth. Not a good time to invest or make big purchases. However, it is a good time to reconnect with an old talent that can eventually, if you invest time and faith, present a new source of income.

 From November 16 to December 6, Mercury retrogrades in Sagittarius and Scorpio. This Mercury can cause misunderstandings and snags in your workplace, with employees, as well as with your health and diet. Your routine and schedule can be interrupted. Make sure no one is stealing or lying at work.

 CANCER

Unpredictable Journey

In 2010, Uranus, the planet of chaos, unpredictability, and revolutions, moved into Aries, the ruler of your house of career. For 7 years, Uranus was causing unpredictable events and disruptive situations in your professional life. On the other hand, it forced you to upgrade and update your workspace, allowing you to keep up with modern trends.

On May 16, 2018, Uranus moves into Taurus, it is not too bad for you as a Cancer. You do need security, and Uranus does not provide it, but since Taurus is a compatible sign, this means that you might enjoy the shakeup and change presented by the joker. Uranus will be in your house of friends and community until 2026. You might make new friends that are funny and somewhat crazy. In addition, Uranus might create a change in the organizations, companies, or communities you belong to. You have to embrace the change and move on. Don't hold onto things too tightly as your fingers might get broken, metaphorically speaking.

Uranus can also present a good time to update and upgrade yourself, connect or invest in startups, and allow more technology, freedom, and originality into your life.

CANCER

Mars Retrograde

Mars is the planet of action, passion, and movement. It is your nuclear reactor. It is your solar panel and battery. It is also the planet ruling seeds and vegetation. Since not all of us are farmers, it translates to whatever projects, creation, and enterprises we plan and sow in our lives. When Mars is retrograding (June 26 to August 27), these aspects of life don't work so well. Metaphorically speaking, these fields we tend don't yield good crops. That does not mean nothing will happen. Sometimes it is actually good to walk backwards. Think of the reverse gear in your car. Where would you be without it? How would you ever be able to park or adjust your position?

During Mars retrograde, you can revisit old projects, make peace, reconnect to past brothers- and sisters-in-arms, reexamine your sexuality and passion, as well as undergo a great deal of healing. As is the rule with all retrograde planets, during the retro period it is safe to engage in any activity that has the prefix re – redo, revert, reject, etc. However, it is not recommended to buy big machinery (cars, appliances) or start a war or a lawsuit (whoever shoots first loses). It is not a good time to start a sexual relationship or launch a big project. Not the best for surgery (unless absolutely needed). Try not to be reactive or overly self-protective, especially during Mercury retro that overlaps Mars retro between July 26 and August 18.

 CANCER

Mars retrogrades in Aquarius, June 26 until August 13. This activates your house of sexuality, death, and transformation. Just like with the eclipses, you will be asked to deal with some loss and release. It is not a good time for investments. You can reexamine your passion. What drives you? What motivates you? Be extra careful with insurance, taxes, or any fines.

 From August 13 to August 27, Mars retrogrades in Capricorn in your house of relationships. This can cause frustration and difficulties with partners and lawsuits. Remember not to start any fights. Past relationships might reappear, but this does not mean you have to be with those partners again.

In September, once Mars goes direct, a great deal of projects that were held back can start flowing better. It will especially be a good time to heal broken relationships and resolve conflicts through compromises.

 ## Venus: Money and Love

Venus is the ruler of comfort, luxury, finance, talents, values, art, and relationships. She is also associated with Maat, the goddess of justice and law.

Venus works in beauty cycles: the more you love yourself, the more you believe in yourself. The better your self-image, the

more you connect to your talents. The more you develop and invest in your talents, the more money you can make. Venus' message is: love yourself and money will follow. Some, however, think that the more money they make, the more they would love themselves and that is a mistake. This year during Venus retrograde (October 6 – November 16), you will be able to change your attitude and fix your relationship to money.

This year Venus will retrograde between October 6 to November 16. First Venus retrogrades in Scorpio (October 6-31), and then she will retrograde in Libra (October 31 – Nov 16). When Venus retrogrades in Scorpio, it is easier for you as Scorpio is a fellow water sign. But still, a retro is a retro, and it can affect your finances, your investments, and your passion. In general, avoid forming any partnerships and, if possible, don't make big investments or purchases. Venus is retrograding in your house of children and love. It can cause challenges and misunderstandings or extra spending with your kids or lovers. When Venus retrogrades in Libra, it can create challenges, but it can also teach profound lessons about relationships and partnerships, especially in your home and with your family.

Venus retro can also show you who your true allies and real enemies are. Since Venus also rules value, it is a good time to review and change your attitudes, aspirations, and values. Venus retro is actually a great time to buy second hand goods. It is also a good time to sell things you don't need. However, if you have secret love affairs, this is the time most of them are discovered.

 CANCER

Venus is in your sign between May 19 and June 13 making you far more attractive to others. It is a great time for romance, making money and connecting to your artistic side. This is a good time for you to rebrand yourself, dress differently, change your hair, get some new clothes. Not a bad time to indulge and pamper yourself (as long as it is healthy and does not harm you or anyone else).

Conclusion:

This is a year of love and relationships. You are a compassionate creature, and 2018 will bring a great deal of opportunities to work on your emotional side by bringing sometimes great and sometimes awful relationships into your life. Compassion does not mean you have to be with or do business with anyone that crosses your path. Be open but selective.

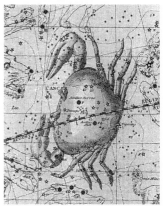

CANCER

23RD JULY – 22ND AUGUST

LEO

*Carried away by a moonlight shadow**

key phrase
I WILL

element
Fixed (unchangeable) fire

planet
The Sun

day
Sunday

incentive
Dynasty

body parts
Heart and spine

color
Golden and yellow

stone
Tiger eye

---

* Mike Oldfield, 1983.

LEO

 Unruly children? Problems in love? Hard to find happiness or feeling like your mojo abandoned you? Well, that was the past. The last couple of years was rough with love for many of you lions. Saturn, the planet of karma and harsh lessons, was in your house of love, happiness, creativity, and children. You were forced to look deeply into these issues and gain clarity by diving deep into the underworld. Saturn teaches us through crisis. In the last three years, you were like the lion in the Wizard of Oz, but soon you can become Aslan, the great savior lion from *The Chronicles of Narnia*, or at least Simba from *The Lion King*.

2017 was not easy for you, since the eclipses shifted into your sign and, around your birthday (August 7 and 21 of 2017), things were heading on a collision course. As you will see below, next year the eclipses are still in your sign and will make life feel faster than normal, but Saturn moving into your house of work, diet, and health will release the blocks that were around your love and children. So yes, love will be easy, but Saturn never tires of teaching us about something we need to fix.

In the next few years, Saturn will fix your work, health, diet, service, and routine. Since it also the house of pets, maybe it is a good idea to pay more attention to them or, if you always wanted to add an animal to your kingdom, 2018 is a good year to do so.

From 2018, for nearly 3 years, Saturn will bring about situations that can rectify the way you serve your body (diet), the

LEO ♌

way you serve others (work), the way others serve you (employees), and the way time serves you (routine). The next few years will be focused on transitions with work. Are you happy with your work or your workspace? If you have your own business or if you are in a managerial position, how are your employees serving you or the company? In the next few years, you will be asked to fix all of this. 2018 is a great year for a detox or for a cleanse. A great time to start a diet, go vegan, start juicing, or eat better.

 With Saturn's strict, stark, and serious nature, Jupiter comes with some good news. Last year, Jupiter was helping you heal, expand, and focus on your siblings as well as writing, business, and contracts. In 2018, you will experience Jupiter's benevolence in your house of home and family. It is a great time to invest in real-estate, move to a more comfortable house, get pregnant, get married, and create a family. There is a possibility for healing relationships or feuds in your family of origin. In general, Jupiter in your house of home can help you be in touch with your feelings and create a better sense of security.

From the second week of November, Jupiter, the benevolent planet and giver of gifts, will move into your house of love and children and will stay there for 12 months! If you want to have children, it is a great time. If you are looking for love, well, it is coming.

♌ LEO

The 5 Eclipses – Your Emotional Landscape

Eclipses quicken processes and push events towards completion. 2018 is a year that will make you feel life is moving faster. You can expect more synchronicities and accelerated stories woven around you.

Once in 18/19 years, the eclipses return to your sign, and this year, like in 2017, the eclipses are hosted by you, Leo, and your opposite sign, Aquarius. You can go back to 1998/1999 and 1980 and see how they synchronized your life in those years. But having eclipses in your sign is not easy. You are a Fire Bender and you like to control life. However, during eclipses, someone else is driving your car. It is best not to overload yourself, your schedule, your work, or your training around the eclipses.

The lunar eclipse on January 31 is in Leo/ Aquarius. Since the moon will be in your sign in this eclipse, it can affect your health, body, and image in your community. Don't be reactive. Try not to roar and be over the top. Since your opposite sign is also activated, it means there could be some ups and downs with your partner or relationships. So breathe deeply and engage in some physical activity to let off some steam.

The solar eclipse on February 15 is centered in the house of relationships and marriage. Since it is the Chinese New Year, it could mean that the next year will be focused around your rela-

LEO ♌

tionships and partners. Since eclipses are unpredictable, and this one is in your house of relationships, it can create enemies and lawsuits. So please be careful the whole month.

 The solar eclipse on July 13 is much more emotional as it is happening in Cancer and takes place in your house of letting go, pain, hospitals, and retreats. I recommend spending this eclipse in a retreat or in nature somewhere close to a water source. It will ask you to cut something out of your life and maybe deal with some loss or grief.

 The lunar eclipse on July 27 is the biblical celebration of love. The moon will be in your house of relationships and marriage. You can see it is a theme this year—me versus us, mine versus yours. Do something special with your partner in work or in life. If you don't have a partner, this is the best day to send a message to the universe that you are truly ready for your twin flame.

 The solar eclipse of August 11 falls in your sign. It will put the moon and the sun together in your house of body and identity. It is a good time for a makeover, for rebranding yourself, or making a fresh start in your life. Watch your body and health around this time, especially with injuries.

♌ LEO

Mercury Retrograde – Mental Landscape

During Mercury retrograde, it is not recommended to start new long-term projects, sign documents, make large purchases, get married, publish, start marketing campaigns, or release new products. Communications of all sorts are slower and filled with glitches and challenges. Computers crash, stock markets turn volatile, flights are delayed, traffic is worse than usual, accidents occur more often, and Murphy's Law takes hold of our lives. For example, the infamous Flash Crash of May 6, 2010, took place during Mercury Retrograde in Taurus (the sign of money and the stock market).

If you must start a new project, be as mindful as you can. Pay attention to small details and read in-between the lines if you must sign a document. Rewrite your emails, edit your texts and think before you speak. In fact, it is better if you spend more time listening than talking. Life does not come to a halt during Mercury retrograde. You can still achieve a great deal. Mercury retro is like going on a vacation while it is raining. It is still possible but not much fun. However, it is a great time to edit, redo, reexamine yourself and your path, revisit old projects, and find lost objects. It is said that there are more coincidences and more synchronicities when Mercury is retrograding. Try to focus on activities that have the prefix *re* – reevaluate, reedit, redo, reexamine, reconnect, regenerate, revisit, re-imagine, etc.

LEO ♌

This year, Mercury retrogrades in fire signs. As you are a Fire Bender, it will not be as tough as it will be for the rest of the signs. But since Mercury will be retrograding in your sign between July 26 and August 18, if your birthday falls in that period, it can get rough. Don't be surprised if no one throws you a surprise party.

Between March 22 and April 15, Mercury retrogrades in Aries, which rules your house of travel, truth, and education. There could be some glitches if you travel abroad (doesn't mean you cannot travel, just be careful). If you are studying, it can be a bit more confusing or you might find it harder to focus on your education. It can also cause misunderstandings with certain in-laws. Since Mercury will be traversing your house of truth, be careful of lies or liars.

Between July 26 and August 18, Mercury retrogrades in your own sign. Boy will you roar! The fact that it is retrograding in your first house might mean that you will be forgetful, give the wrong impression, have a lot of slips of tongue, etc. Make sure to do some cardio or breathe deeply since Mercury rules air.

From November 16 to December 6, Mercury is retrograding in Sagittarius and Scorpio. This can cause misunderstandings and miscommunications with children or lovers. Be careful of sports injuries.

♌ LEO

Unpredictable Journey

In 2010, Uranus, the planet of chaos, unpredictability, and revolutions moved into Aries, the ruler of your house of education, foreign cultures, and truth. It made it rather chaotic with in-laws, caused some unpredictability when you traveled, and attracted a great deal of questionable people into your life. It also shook your philosophies and creeds. Suddenly, you were not sure what your core beliefs were. But now all this is over. Travel will be less chaotic and education as well as publishing will be easier.

 In May, Uranus moves into Taurus, and that would make May-August a bit uncertain and hard to plan. Uranus in Taurus is not comfortable for you as Taurus is a fellow fixed sign, and that means you are squaring each other. You would rather control things and know the protocol, but when Uranus is in Taurus the only protocol is that there is none. Uranus will be in your house of career, figures of authority, and status until about 2026. All these aspects of your life are very important for you as a Leo, but in the next few years, you will have to be okay with sudden changes in direction. If your career is a highway, well, some of the ramps are going to be closed, and a great deal of rerouting will take place.

Uranus can also ask you to make a leap of faith into a new field. It is time to look at ways you can implement and invoke new technology and innovation to your professional life. Go to professional conferences. Subscribe to trade magazine or

LEO ♌

newsletters that can inform you about the future of your field. It is a great time to upgrade your career, work on your digital representation (social media, web site). It is beneficial to incorporate younger, creative, ingenious, and original-thinking people into your career path. Uranus is revolution and freedom, and you need both of those aspects in your career right now.

However, since the house of career is also the house of the father, boss, or authority figure, Uranus in that house can cause disruption with these people. Try to be humorous and original in your career or in your dealings with them. The key words for success: "no fear"!

 ## Mars Retrograde

Mars is the planet of action, passion, and movement. It is your nuclear reactor. It is your solar panel and battery. It is also the planet ruling seeds and vegetation. Since not all of us are farmers, it translates to whatever projects, creation, and enterprises we plan and sow in our lives. When Mars is retrograding (June 26 to August 27), these aspects of life don't work so well. Metaphorically speaking, these fields we tend don't yield good crops. That does not mean nothing will happen. Sometime it is actually good to walk backwards. Think of the reverse gear in your car. Where would you be without it? How would you ever be able to park or adjust your position?

During Mars retrograde you can revisit old projects, make peace, reconnect to past brothers- and sisters-in-arms, reex-

♌ LEO

amine your sexuality and passion, as well as undergo a great deal of healing. As is the rule with all retrograde planets, during the retro period it is safe to engage in any activity that has the prefix re – redo, revert, reject, etc. However, it is not recommended to buy big machinery (cars, appliances) or start a war or a lawsuit (whoever shoots first loses). It is not a good time to start a sexual relationship or launch a big project. Not the best for surgery (unless absolutely needed). Try not to be reactive or overly self-protective, especially during Mercury retro that overlaps Mars retro between July 26 and August 18.

Mars retrogrades in Aquarius between June 26 and August 13. This is your opposite sign and, as we saw before, falls in your house of marriage and enemies. It can cause arguments, breakups, as well as unnecessary wars and lawsuits. Please understand that you might come across as over-controlling and authoritative. Lower the volume of your roars. And remember, don't start wars. But if others start one, god help them, you can then be the feline you are and put them in their place.

Mars retrogrades in Capricorn between August 13 and August 27. This will take place in your house of health and diet. Please watch what you eat and also be careful with some of your co-workers and employees. Your schedule might be out of whack. Try to be flexible. Even your pets might seem a bit off. However, from September, once Mars goes direct, a great deal of projects that were held back can start flowing better especially at work. Even your health can improve.

LEO ♌

Venus: Money and Love

Venus is the ruler of comfort, luxury, finance, talents, values, art, and relationships. She is also associated with Maat, the goddess of justice and law.

Venus works in beauty cycles: the more you love yourself, the more you believe in yourself. The better your self-image, the more you connect to your talents. The more you develop and invest in your talents, the more money you can make. Venus' message is: love yourself and money will follow. Some, however, think that the more money they make, the more they would love themselves and that is a mistake. This year during Venus retrograde (October 6 – November 16), you will be able to change your attitude and fix your relationship to money.

This year, Venus will retrograde between October 6 and November 16. First Venus retrogrades in Scorpio (October 6-31), and then she will retrograde in Libra (October 31 – Nov 16). When Venus is retrograding in Scorpio, she can affect your finances, your investments, and your passion. In general, avoid forming any partnerships and, if possible, don't make big investments or purchases. Venus is retrograding in your house of home and family. You can expect some additional expenses in your home or some strife in relationships in the family. Not a good time to buy appliances.

♌ LEO

When Venus retrogrades in Libra, it can create challenges but also profound lessons in relationships and partnerships, especially with siblings, relatives, and neighbors. Pay extra attention to contracts.

Since Venus also rules value, it is a good time to review and change your attitudes, aspirations, and values. Venus retro is actually a great time to buy second hand goods. It is also a good time to sell things you don't need. However, if you have secret love affairs, this is the time most of them are discovered.

Venus is in your sign between June 13 and July 10, making you far more attractive to others. It is a great time for romance, making money, and connecting to your artistic side. This is a good time for you to rebrand yourself, dress differently, change your hair, and get some new clothes. Not a bad time to indulge and pamper yourself (as long as it is healthy and does not harm you or anyone else).

Conclusion:

This is a year where you have to focus on your work, diet, health, and service. But because the eclipses are in your sign, it is a year of a great deal of swings in love and relationships. It is safe to say 2018 is an exciting and entertaining year, which you would love!

LEO ♌

23RD AUGUST – 22ND SEPTEMBER

VIRGO ♍

When I'm feeling sad, I simply remember my favorite things, and then I don't feel so bad*

key phrase
I SERVE

element
Mutable (changeable) earth

planet
Mercury

day
Wednesday

incentive
Making things happen

body parts
Intestines, colon

color
Yellow-green

stone
Agate

---

* The Sound of Music, 1959.

♍ VIRGO

 The last few years were not easy on the home front. Saturn, the lord of karma and provider of tough lessons, was in your house of home, family, motherhood, and security. You are typically very analytical and logical, but the last few years were emotional, and you were forced to walk in uncharted territories. In addition, the eclipses in 2015 and 2016 were in your sign and caused a great deal of upheaval and change. Many Virgos reevaluated their family status. Some even divorced. Some changed location. And some committed to buying property. Saturn is not evil. It teaches us what we don't want to learn. It is the kind of personal trainer who, while he makes us throw up, also manages to banish the extra weight.

This year Saturn is moving into your house of love, children, and happiness. Now Saturn will ask you questions such as: where is your love? What moves you in life? What is your hobby—wait, do you have one? Are you having fun? What happened to your inner child? What are your relationships with your kids? Again, Saturn is not an agent of the devil. Saturn is the contractor here to fix us and make us better. Saturn in the house of children can bring issues with your children or with the children of your mind, as in your baby projects. Maybe you will start feeling that whatever was causing you happiness before does not work anymore. Some people quit recreational drugs or partying during this transit. So that is not a bad transit at all.

On the more positive side, you might decide to embark on a new hobby or a new sport that can bring a great deal of joy into your life. Saturn can also help you break away from old patterns in love, and it might do so by bringing past lovers back into your life to test or even tempt you. Virgos love to learn, and your sign is the sign of methodology and structure. Saturn will give you all of this if you allow him to work for you. I know it sounds weird, but you have to be disciplined with your happiness. Maybe you can read some books about positive psychology or some scientific research concerning happiness.

With Saturn's strict, stark, and serious nature, Jupiter comes with some good news. Last year, Jupiter was helping you connect to your talents, finances, and self-worth. Many Virgos got awards and recognition. And even if you didn't get a promotion or a raise, don't think you missed the boat. Some seeds were planted in 2017 that will bring fruition in the next few years.

 This year, Jupiter is moving into your house of communication, business, and marketing. 2018 is a great year for publishing, writing, connecting, and being connected. If you had any quarrels or issues with relatives, siblings, or neighbors, it is the year you can bring some peace and resolution. There also might be some good news regarding a sibling or nephews, nieces, and cousins. After a few emotional years, you are finally back to the familiar realm of reason and the mind.

From the second week of November, Jupiter, the benevolent planet and giver of gifts, will move into your house of home and family for 12 months. Great time to buy a property, get pregnant, and heal familial relationships.

♍ VIRGO

The 5 Eclipses –
Your Emotional Landscape

Eclipses quicken processes and push events towards completion. 2018 is a year that will make you feel life is moving faster. You can expect more synchronicities and accelerated stories woven around you.

The eclipses this year fall in the axis of Leo/Aquarius. This is not easy for you, as you are an Earth Bender and neither fire nor air are compatible with earth. But you can make it work with a little alchemy. For fire, you need to be more active. For air, you need to try to be more communicative.

The lunar eclipse of January 31 falls in your house of past lifetimes, letting go, pain and suffering, as well as the house of work and health. It sounds a bit morbid, but it does not have to be that way. If you let go, surrender, and accept what life offers or takes away, you might actually benefit from this intense eclipse.

The solar eclipse on February 15 is focused in the house of work, health, and diet. It can create an acceleration in whatever is happening in your workspace or whatever is going on with your diet. There might be some revelations regarding co-workers or employees. Like in the case of the former eclipse, pay attention to your health and diet. It is a great time to go to a nutritionist and look into allergies.

VIRGO

The solar eclipse on July 13 is far easier for you to handle as it is in Cancer, a water sign that can sprinkle some compassion into your life. The eclipse takes place in your house of friends and community. There could be some change with your company or organization. Maybe a friend will need your help or expose some unpleasant truth. I recommend spending the eclipse in the company of close friends that feel like family and doing something close to a water source like an ocean, pool, jacuzzi, spa, lake, or river.

 The lunar eclipse on July 27 is the biblical celebration of love. The moon will be in your house of work and health and the sun in your house of previous lives. Again, watch your health. Make sure to boost your immune system. But this eclipse can also bring you a love from a past lifetime or a skill you might have had in a previous life. It is great day for meditation and or yoga outdoors.

 The solar eclipse of August 11 is in your house of spirituality and past lifetimes. Start something new in your spiritual practice even though it is a Mercury retrograde.

♍ VIRGO

Mercury Retrograde – Mental Landscape

While Mercury is retrograding, you experience the cosmic mental breakdown more severely than other signs. We always rely on you, Virgo, to deliver our messages and explain the sordid details of lives to us but, when your planet is on strike, you feel helpless and we get confused.

During Mercury retrograde, it is not recommended to start new long-term projects, sign documents, make large purchases, get married, publish, start marketing campaigns, or release new products. Communications of all sorts are slower and filled with glitches and challenges. Computers crash, stock markets turn volatile, flights are delayed, traffic is worse than usual, accidents occur more often, and Murphy's Law takes hold of our lives. For example, the infamous Flash Crash of May 6, 2010, took place during Mercury Retrograde in Taurus (the sign of money and the stock market).

If you must start a new project, be as mindful as you can. Pay attention to small details and read in-between the lines if you must sign a document. Rewrite your emails, edit your texts, and think before you speak. In fact, it is better if you spend more time listening than talking. Life does not come to a halt during Mercury retrograde. You can still achieve a great deal. Mercury retro is like going on a vacation while it is raining. It is still possible but not much fun. However, it is a great time to edit, redo, reexamine yourself and your path, revisit old pro-

VIRGO

jects, and find lost objects. It is said that there are more coincidences and more synchronicities when Mercury is retrograding. Try to focus on activities that have the prefix re – reevaluate, reedit, redo, reexamine, reconnect, regenerate, revisit, re-imagine, etc. After all, Virgo is the sign of editing, so it is not all terrible news for you during retrograding Mercury.

This year, Mercury is retrograding in fire signs, which is not always comfortable for you. Virgo is like the super nanny and fire signs are little brats you will have to govern during these periods.

 From March 22 to April 15, Mercury is retrograding in Aries. This Mercury retrograde is in your house of sexuality, death, transformation, investments, and the occult. It is the underworld. You see that this year forces you to deal with your shadow. You are asked to go to dark places that you usually prefer to avoid. This retrograde is not a good time to invest or start a new sexual relationship. Some old fears or traumas can surface, but Mercury is the healer, and you can use this period for therapy. It is a good time to connect to spirits, pray, make wishes come true, and use magic to heal ancient wounds.

 From July 26 to August 18, Mercury retrogrades in Leo, the sign that is in your house of past lifetimes. Maybe you will meet someone who has known you in a previous life when you were famous or a celebrity and reminds you of your inner gloriousness. You might find something that was lost or hidden from you.

♍ VIRGO

From November 16 to December 6, Mercury is retrograding in Sagittarius and Scorpio. This can cause misunderstandings with family members or around real estate. Not a good time to buy any property or start renovations.

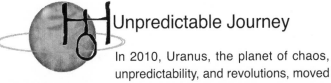 ## Unpredictable Journey

In 2010, Uranus, the planet of chaos, unpredictability, and revolutions, moved into Aries. This means that, in the last 7 years, you experienced a great deal of fluctuations and changes with taxes, insurance, inheritance, death, and sexuality. Sexuality? Yes, even the Virgin gets to explore intimacy. You were asked to be experimental with all these aspects, and it was not comfortable. It could also have caused some disruption with your finances and sense of security.

 In May, when Uranus moves into Taurus, it is not so bad for you. Taurus is a fellow earth sign and this means you might get a good push, especially if you are open to connecting to technology and younger innovative people. Uranus will be in your house of travel and education until about 2026. This is a great time to upgrade and update yourself, connect to technology, especially coming from foreign cultures or through foreigners. Uranus can also represent a leap of faith into a new exciting field of study. It can also bring technology and innovation into your life.

VIRGO

It is a great year to go back to school and study something practical that can help you either serve better, get a promotion at work, or become healthier. The more unique, original, wild, crazy, and futuristic the field of study, the better!

Mars Retrograde

Mars is the planet of action, passion, and movement. It is your nuclear reactor. It is your solar panel and battery. It is also the planet ruling seeds and vegetation. Since not all of us are farmers, it translates to whatever projects, creations, and enterprises we plan and sow in our lives. When Mars is retrograding (June 26 to August 27), these aspects of life don't work so well. Metaphorically speaking, these fields we tend don't yield good crops. That does not mean nothing will happen. Sometime it is actually good to walk backward. Think of the reverse gear in your car. Where would you be without it? How would you ever be able to park or adjust your position?

During Mars retrograde, you can revisit old projects, make peace, reconnect to past brothers- and sisters-in-arms, reexamine your sexuality and passion, as well as undergo a great deal of healing. As is the rule with all retrograde planets, during the retro period it is safe to engage in any activity that has the prefix re – redo, revert, reject, etc. However, it is not recommended to buy big machinery (cars, appliances) or start a war or a lawsuit (whoever shoots first loses). It is not a good time to start a sexual relationship or launch a big project. Not the best for surgery (unless absolutely needed). Try not to be reactive or overly self-protective, especially during Mercury retro that overlaps Mars retro between July 26 and August 18.

 Mars retrogrades in Aquarius from June 26 until August 13. This takes place in your house of health. As you can see, your health is a recurring theme this year. Mars retro is also associated with injuries and mishaps. Watch where you are going and don't look at the ground or at your mobile phone when you are walking. Pay attention to your diet and allergies. Since the house of health is also the house of pets, be more mindful with your furry friends. Also, Mars can cause conflict with co-workers and employees. Chose your wars wisely.

 When Mars retrogrades in Capricorn, between August 13 and August 27, it will be easier, since Capricorn is a fellow earth sign. This will take place in your house of love and creativity. It is a good time to review creative projects and connect to recreational activities you might have enjoyed in the past. But since it is Mars retro, be careful of injuries. This retro can also cause conflict with your children, or it can possibly result in your kids getting sick or injured. Please be patient with them and with yourself. However, from September, once Mars goes direct, a great deal of projects that were held back can start flowing better, especially with your creative endeavors, children, love, and general sense of happiness.

VIRGO ♍

Venus: Money and Love

Venus is the ruler of comfort, luxury, finance, talents, values, art, and relationships. She is also associated with Maat, the goddess of justice and law.

Venus works in beauty cycles: the more you love yourself, the more you believe in yourself. The better your self-image, the more you connect to your talents. The more you develop and invest in your talent, the more money you can make. Venus message is: love yourself and money will follow. Some, however, think that the more money they make, the more they would love themselves and that is a mistake. This year during Venus retrograde (October 6 – November 16), you will be able to change your attitude and fix your relationship to money.

 This year, Venus will retrograde between October 6 and November 16. First, Venus retrogrades in Scorpio (October 6-31), and then she will retrograde in Libra (October 31 – Nov 16). When Venus is retrograding in Scorpio, she can affect your finances, your investments, and your passion. She can also create problems with contracts, roommates, marketing, and siblings. In general, avoid forming any partnerships and, if possible, don't make big investments or purchases. When Venus retrogrades in Libra, it can create challenges but also profound lessons in relationships and part-

nerships. It can also jeopardize your self-worth, self-esteem, and earning potential.

Venus retro can also show you who your true allies and real enemies are. Since Venus also rules value, it is a good time to review and change your attitudes, aspirations, and values. Venus retro is actually a great time to buy second hand goods. It is also a good time to sell things you don't need. However, if you have secret love affairs, this is the time most of them are discovered.

Venus is in your sign between July 10 and August 6, making you far more attractive to others. It is a great time for romance, making money, and connecting to your artistic side. This is a good time for you to rebrand yourself, dress differently, change your hair, and get some new clothes. Not a bad time to indulge and pamper yourself (as long as it is healthy and does not harm you or anyone else).

Conclusion:

This year you are visiting your shadow, looking into your spirituality, and getting a great deal of messages from past lifetimes. It is exciting! Watch your health, make changes in your diet and focus on preventive medicine. Also, it is the Year of the Dog and all that activity in your house of pets means you may need one. Enjoy the ride and don't over analyze.

VIRGO

LIBRA ♎

Country roads, take me home, to the place I belong*

key phrase
I BALANCE

element
Cardinal air

planet
Venus

day
Friday

incentive
Mirror of love affairs

body parts
Kidneys, waist, ovaries

color
Green

stone
Opal

---

* John Denver, 1971.

♎ LIBRA

 Saturn, known in Kabbalah as the rectifier, the fixer, teaches us with the stick rather than the carrot. In the last few years, Saturn was trying to teach you how to communicate better. It is strange, as Libra is a cardinal air sign, which means you can teach the rest of the zodiac how to interconnect. But even a doctor has to go to visit a doctor and a teacher also needs to learn. The last few years were focused on education, writing, and testing to see how well you communicate. It was not easy to make decisions (worse than usual), and you might have experienced some issues with siblings, roommates, neighbors, and relatives. But this is over. The next few years Saturn will be in your house of home and family, moving you from the kingdom of the mind into the queendom of the heart.

Saturn teachings in the house of family have to do with finding your sense of security. Where and with whom do you feel safe? This is the time that many Libras will experience their home life falling apart, while others will create a family. It is a good time to commit and buy a property, change location, get pregnant, and heal relationships with family members, especially mothers. Saturn is not good or bad. It simply brings to the light what needs to be rectified.

Saturn would like you to feel and emote more. It will probe and seek what moves you emotionally. For this reason, you might feel uncomfortable, especially around the eclipses. If you ever wanted to create a family or commit to a serious relationship, 2018 is your year to make it happen.

LIBRA ♎

With Saturn's strict, stark, and serious nature, Jupiter comes with some good news. Last year, Jupiter was traveling in your sign for the first time in 12 years (September 2016 to October 2017). This should have brought you some interesting opportunities and should have opened doors in many areas of your life. Now Jupiter is in your house of money, talents, and self-worth. In 2018, you will discover new talents that can potentially become a money source. You might get an award or the well-deserved recognition you desire as well as a raise and or a promotion. Who knows, maybe all of the above. Be careful not to be over-generous and spend too much money on yourself or others. Yes, this year you can increase your earning potential, but it will be wise to save it.

From the second week of November, Jupiter, the benevolent planet and giver of gifts, will move into your house of communication, writing, and contracts for 12 months. Expect lucrative contracts and better relationships with relatives. Great time for marketing.

The 5 Eclipses – Your Emotional Landscape

Eclipses quicken processes and push events towards completion. 2018 is a year that will make you feel life is moving faster. You can expect more synchronicities and accelerated stories woven around you.

The eclipses in 2018 fall on the Leo/Aquarius axis. These signs are easy for you to work with. After all, you are an Air Bender and the flames of Leo help you climb higher while Aquarius is your fellow air sign. This means you can channel the lunations with more ease than other signs.

 The lunar eclipse of January 31 creates an opposition and maybe a conflict between your love and your friends or between your children and company. The moon falls in your house of friends, corporations, and government while the sun shines your house of love and happiness. This is not a bad alignment but it could cause some friction and opposition between what you feel and what you think, between your desires and your duty. Try to balance both aspects of your life to insure harmony between all those you love and who love you.

 The solar eclipse on February 15 is focused in the house of love and children. This is the Chinese New Year, and it can color the whole year with the golden hues of love and happiness and maybe a new baby. But as we know, eclipses are unpredictable. If you have kids they might go through some transi-

LIBRA

tions and, if you don't, maybe a new "baby" project will come out of your mental womb.

 The solar eclipse on July 13 is emotional as it is happening in Cancer, which is not a comfortable sign for you. But it is the sign that rules home and family, which is what you want to focus on this year. The eclipse falls in your house of career, which means that you will be forced into action in your career probably instigated by a father figure or a boss. Try to balance your emotion with your reason and try not to choose one over the other.

 The lunar eclipse on July 27, which happens right on the biblical day of love, falls in your houses of love and friends. What a synchronicity! It increases the chances for love and happiness! If you are married, be careful of extramarital affairs. If you are not, it might mean that love is coming to your heart or maybe a new hobby or a recreational activity is incorporated into your life.

 The solar eclipse of August 11 is in your house of friends and companies. It could mean a new offer from a group or a corporation. Processes are quickened around governments, organizations, and nonprofits. It is a good time to make wishes come true and manifest your desires.

♎ LIBRA

Mercury Retrograde – Mental Landscape

During Mercury retrograde, it is not recommended to start new long-term projects, sign documents, make large purchases, get married, publish, start marketing campaigns, or release new products. Communications of all sorts are slower and filled with glitches and challenges. Computers crash, stock markets turn volatile, flights are delayed, traffic is worse than usual, accidents occur more often, and Murphy's Law takes hold of our lives. For example, the infamous Flash Crash of May 6, 2010, took place during Mercury Retrograde in Taurus (the sign of money and the stock market).

If you must start a new project, be as mindful as you can. Pay attention to small details and read in-between the lines if you must sign a document. Rewrite your emails, edit your texts, and think before you speak. In fact, it is better if you spend more time listening than talking. Life does not come to a halt during Mercury retrograde. You can still achieve a great deal. Mercury retro is like going on a vacation while it is raining. It is still possible but not much fun. However, it is a great time to edit, redo, reexamine yourself and your path, revisit old projects, and find lost objects. It is said that there are more coincidences and more synchronicities when Mercury is retrograding. Try to focus on activities that have the prefix *re* – reevaluate, reedit, redo, reexamine, reconnect, regenerate, revisit, re-imagine, etc.

LIBRA

This year, Mercury is retrograding in fire signs, which is actually good for you since, as you know, you are an air sign. But all that fire might make you write and speak faster and therefore be more prone to slips of tongue and other unfortunate miscommunications.

Between March 22 and April 15, Mercury is retrograding in Aries, your opposite and complimentary sign. This Mercury retrograde falls in your house of relationships and marriage. You will experience some chaos around your partners in life or work. Be extra careful, since it is also the house of enemies. During this retrograde, small conflicts can escalate into huge fights. Do what you do best. Be a diplomat and use your lawyer skills.

From July 26 to August 18, Mercury retrogrades in Leo. This could manifest as glitches, delays, and problems with permits, taxes, letters from governments, and issues with friends or corporations. Maybe someone you have not seen for a long time will return to your life.

From November 16 to December 6, Mercury is retrograding in Sagittarius and Scorpio. This falls in your house of communication and money. Since Mercury is the messenger, you have to watch what you say and write. Make sure you read contracts or documents three times before you sign anything. Be extra forgiving to relatives and siblings. It is a dangerous time for investments.

 LIBRA

Unpredictable Journey

In 2010, Uranus, the planet of chaos, unpredictability, and revolutions, moved into Aries. Since Aries is your opposite sign, it serves as your mirror, your soul-mate, and your best teacher. Having Uranus in your house of marriage was not easy as you are the sign of relationship. For 7 years, it felt like there was no justice, life was not fair, and it was hard to find balance. Uranus was causing your partnerships to feel like a roller-coaster ride with crazy twists and turns. You attracted strange people into your life, and many of your partners in work or in life demanded too much freedom or maybe you wanted more space in your relationships. But now this is changing as Uranus flies away from your house of relationships and dives deep into the underworld...

From May 2018, Uranus will move into your house of sexuality, intimacy, death, and transformation. Uranus is very experimental, and he always strives to bring strange, ingenious, quirky, and rebellious people into your life. In one sense, Uranus in the house of sexuality can liberate your passion and make you open up to different types of sexual expression, but it can also be disruptive and unpredictable. Let's play safe and agree to explore, but let's not jump off the cliff into an erotic abyss.

Uranus can bring an unexpected investment, especially in a project that has to do with technology, innovation, startups, social media, and science. In addition, you will find that

LIBRA

laughter and humor could be great healers. Uranus can open your horizon until 2026 if you accept change, innovation, and originality into your life. Come face the strange!

Mars Retrograde

Mars is the planet of action, passion, and movement. It is your nuclear reactor. It is your solar panel and battery. It is also the planet ruling seeds and vegetation. Since not all of us are farmers, it translates to whatever projects, creations, and enterprises we plan and sow in our lives. When Mars is retrograding (June 26 to August 27) these aspects of life don't work so well. Metaphorically speaking, these fields we tend don't yield good crops. That does not mean nothing will happen. Sometime it is actually good to walk backward. Think of the reverse gear in your car. Where would you be without it? How would you ever be able to park or adjust your position?

During Mars retrograde, you can revisit old projects, make peace, reconnect to past brothers- and sisters-in-arms, reexamine your sexuality and passion, as well as undergo a great deal of healing. As is the rule with all retrograde planets, during the retro period it is safe to engage in any activity that has the prefix re – redo, revert, reject, etc. However, it is not recommended to buy big machinery (cars, appliances) or start a war or a lawsuit (whoever shoots first loses). It is not a good time to start a sexual relationship or launch a big project. Not the best for surgery (unless absolutely needed). Try not to be reactive or overly self-protective especially during Mercury retro that overlaps Mars retro between July 26 and August 18.

 Mars retrogrades in Aquarius between June 26 and August 13. This can manifest as conflict with lovers or with your children. It can also create delays in creative projects or cause sports injuries.

 When Mars retrogrades in Capricorn, August 13 to August 27, there might be strife at home or with family members. Make sure you have earthquake and fire insurance if you own your own property and try not to be reactive with family members. Anger management will be a good idea in those two months.

In September, once Mars goes direct, a great deal of projects that were held back can start flowing better. It will be a good time to buy property and heal familial relationships.

 ## Venus: Money and Love

Venus is the ruler of comfort, luxury, finance, talents, values, art, and relationships. She is also associated with Maat, the goddess of justice and law.

Venus works in beauty cycles: the more you love yourself, the more you believe in yourself. The better your self-image, the more you connect to your talents. The more you develop and invest in your talent, the more money you can make. Venus

LIBRA ♎

message is: love yourself and money will follow. Some, however, think that the more money they make, the more they would love themselves and that is a mistake. This year during Venus retrograde (October 6 – November 16), you will be able to change your attitude and fix your relationship to money.

 This year, Venus will retrograde between October 6 and November 16. First, Venus retrogrades in Scorpio (October 6-31), and then she will retrograde in Libra (October 31 – Nov 16). When she is retrograding in Scorpio, she can affect your finances, income, and earning potential. Since Venus is retrograding in your house of money, please be more conservative with your spending. Maybe it is time to start monitoring and balancing spending and earning?

When Venus retrogrades in Libra, your sign, it can be pretty intense in many different aspects of your life. You might come across as aloof or strange. You might feel more withdrawn or sad. But remember it is only a short cycle. You can use it to change the way you dress or look. Maybe change your hair, try wearing different clothes or change your style. It is a good time to redo your web site or your business cards.

This year, Venus, your planet, will be in your sign for a long period, since she is retrograding back and forth in your kingdom. While it is not easy to have Venus retrograde in Libra, it is also great for you! Between August 6 and September 9, Venus will be hosted by Libra and then again between Oct 31 and December 2. Those are a lot of Venus days for you. When Venus is in your sign, you appear far more attractive to others. It is a great time for romance, making money, and connecting to your artistic side. This is a good time for you to rebrand yourself, dress differently, change your hair, and get some new clothes. Not a bad time to indulge and pamper yourself (as long as it is healthy and does not harm you or anyone else).

Conclusion:

Home, family, real-estate, as well as love and happiness, are the most important aspects for you to master and learn. 2018 is a year you will have the ability to change so many things that were stuck and stagnant on the emotional and sexual front. Since you are a social creature and 2018 is not an easy year, you will be called upon to mediate, balance, and act as a peacemaker for a great deal of people in work as well as in your personal life. It is part of your duty. I am certain, for all of our sakes, that you will do a good job at it!

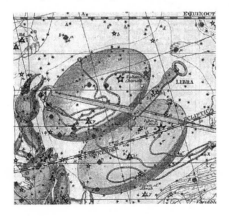

LIBRA ♎

23ʳᴰ OCTOBER – 22ᴺᴰ NOVEMBER

SCORPIO ♏

I feel good, I knew that I would now, so good, so good.*

key phrase
I TRANSFORM

element
Fixed (unchangeable) water

planet
Mars

day
Tuesday

incentive
Regeneration

body parts
Sex organs, reproductive system, nose

color
Turquoise/green-blue

stone
Topaz

---

* James Brown, 1964.

♏ SCORPIO

 In the last few years, Saturn, the Lord Karma and deliverer of harsh lessons, was providing you with opportunities to fix, focus, and rectify your financial situation and self-worth. It was not supposed to be easy. Many Scorpios changed the way they made money. Some invested in their talents. Many more had to deal with financial setbacks. This process was designed to help you restructure your values and help you set your priorities straight. In 2018, you are coming out of the financial swamp and in 2019 abundance is coming your way.

In the last few weeks of 2017, Saturn shifted gears and moved into your house of communication. Yes, we all know that Scorpios are secretive and private folk. You made a name for yourself as being the master spies, the poker players of the zodiac who never show their cards. As a Water Bender you are a mute sign, not because you have nothing to say, but because you rather keep us all on a "need to know basis". But this year, things are changing. Saturn, for the first time in 30 years, will help you look deeply at your communication skills. How do you market yourself? How do you share information? What do you want to communicate to the word? What is your message? If you were a country, it would mean you are fixing your infrastructure.

Saturn can also help you look into how you think, your attitudes, as well as the way you see life. If the last three years were about discovering new ways of connecting to your talents and earning potential, you now have to present them to

SCORPIO ♏

the world and market yourself. As a mute sign, it is not comfortable, but it is necessary.

In the next few years, you will have to reexamine all of your commitments and contracts. It is also a time to look into your business and occupational contacts. There could be some challenges regarding contracts and documents, permits, and red tape. In addition, Saturn's lessons can include some focus on fixing your relationship with siblings, relatives, roommates, and neighbors. This can be especially tougher at the end of the Mars retrograde period in August.

 With Saturn's strict, stark, and serious nature, Jupiter comes with a breath of fresh air. Last year, Jupiter was helping you get rid of things, let go of habits or addictions. It was helping you tap into the mystical and magical. However, this year Jupiter is in your sign! That is the best news you have received in a while. It started mid-October, 2017, and will continue for most of 2018. This transit happens every 12 years, and you can go back to 2006, 1994, and 1982 to try to identify how Jupiter worked with you before.

In general terms, when Jupiter is in your sign, you experience flow and good luck. What is luck? It is synchronicities that open doors and save a lot of time. It is as if you are surfing big waves and you are at one with their flow. Since Jupiter is blessing all aspects of your life, you should start feeling better and better as the year progresses. However, be careful not to feel too good. What I mean is not to overextend yourself, over-commit, be over-optimistic and/or become full of yourself. Jupiter inflates. Make sure it does not inflate your ego.

♏ SCORPIO

Jupiter can help you rebrand yourself as well as reinvent how you are perceived by others. It is a great time to start dressing differently, change your looks, get new business cards, change your picture on social media outlets, and redo your web site. You will feel more attractive and at one with the universe. It is also recommended to start a new physical activity: yoga, martial arts, dance, or a new sport. Hiking? Whatever can give your body an opportunity to grow in a productive and constructive way. The dark side of Jupiter in your sign is gluttony and overindulgence. For every chocolate cake (real or metaphorical), make sure you spend some time in the gym, dojo, or yoga studio.

From the second week of November, Jupiter, the benevolent planet and giver of gifts, will move into your house of money and talents for 12 months. You can expect new sources of income, a raise, and in general, a good flow of money.

 ## The 5 Eclipses – Your Emotional Landscape

Eclipses quicken processes and push events towards completion. 2018 is a year that will make you feel life is moving faster. You can expect more synchronicities and accelerated stories woven around you. The moon is not always easy for you to handle. Even though you are a water sign, the moon is considered fallen when it is in Scorpio. Why? Because you and your tribe are the deepest of them all. If Pisces is the river and Cancer is the lake, then you are the deepest part of the mighty ocean, so deep that it is dark.

On a psychological level, this means that Scorpio carries powerful emotional currents that are not easily understood by others or by themselves.

Scorpio is the sign of transformation. No wonder werewolves, vampires, and creatures of the night are associated with Scorpio. On the lunation (eclipses, full and new moon) the werewolf in you comes out to hunt. For your sake and ours, please be extra careful around the eclipse. It is not all bad, as the eclipses can also give you the ability to transform in a positive way. You can heal, manifest magic, get enlightened, and heal others during eclipses.

The eclipses of 2018 are located in the Leo/Aquarius axis. Both signs are not easy for you to handle or channel. You are a fixed sign and these two signs are also fixed. This is too much fixation in a time you need to be flexible. Around the eclipses, it is a good idea to spend more time on the yoga mat or stretching (your mind as well as body) to gain more fluidity.

 The lunar eclipse of January 31 is creating an opposition between your home and career, between your feelings and your duty. There might be old buried issues in the family that surface. Try not to bring stress from work into your home or vice versa.

The solar eclipse on February 15, the Chinese New Year, is located in your house of home and family. This can color the whole year with emotional hues triggered by your home, mother or motherhood, pregnancies, and family members. A new cycle begins for you in connection to your family life.

♏ SCORPIO

The solar eclipse on July 13 is far easier as it is taking place in Cancer, a fellow Water Bender. It will be located in your house of travel, education, and foreign cultures. It is a good time to start learning a new language or to travel to a place you have not been before.

 The lunar eclipse on July 27 pits your work and family life once again in opposition. Since it is also the biblical "Valentine's", maybe there is new love coming from someone in connection to your career, or maybe a new idea can become your "baby" in relation to a work project.

 The solar eclipse on August 11 is focused on your house and career. This Solar eclipse can launch something new in your career, bringing about extra responsibility or new tasks, but it can also create some tension with a father figure in your life.

 ## Mercury Retrograde – Mental Landscape

During Mercury retrograde, it is not recommended to start new long-term projects, sign documents, make large purchases, get married, publish, start marketing campaigns, or release new products. Communications of all sorts are slower and filled with glitches and challenges. Computers crash, stock markets turn volatile, flights are delayed, traffic is worse than usual, accidents occur more often, and Murphy's Law takes hold of our lives. For example, the infamous Flash

 SCORPIO ♏

Crash of May 6, 2010, took place during Mercury Retrograde in Taurus (the sign of money and the stock market).

If you must start a new project, be as mindful as you can. Pay attention to small details and read in-between the lines if you must sign a document. Rewrite your emails, edit your texts, and think before you speak. In fact, it is better if you spend more time listening than talking. Life does not come to a halt during Mercury retrograde. You can still achieve a great deal. Mercury retro is like going on a vacation while it is raining. It is still possible but not much fun. However, it is a great time to edit, redo, reexamine yourself and your path, revisit old projects, and find lost objects. It is said that there are more coincidences and more synchronicities when Mercury is retrograding. Try to focus on activities that have the prefix re – reevaluate, reedit, redo, reexamine, reconnect, regenerate, revisit, re-imagine, etc.

This year, Mercury is retrograding in fire signs. As a water sign, it might be a bit harder for you to deal with, especially since Mercury is the messenger of the gods and, as we saw earlier, Saturn is in your house of communication. You might lose your temper or write/say/text things you would later regret or regret not regretting. You are in danger of stinging instead of talking, so please take heed and watch what you

♏ SCORPIO

say. Review emails twice before sending them and mind your spellchecker or dictionary when you text!

 Between March 22 and April 15, Mercury is retrograding in Aries. Aries shares the same ruler as you, Mars, which makes you and Aries step-siblings. This retrograde is located in your house of health, diet, pets, and work. These are the areas where snags and glitches can occur more often. Make sure you are patient with employees and co-workers. If you have pets, be nice to them as Mercury can cause misunderstandings with them as well. Be careful not to push people's buttons at work. On the health front, watch your diet. Maybe some allergies could flare up.

 Between July 26 and August 18, Mercury retrogrades in Leo. This takes place in your career. Miscommunications with authority figures or with your father. Too much ego, excessive volume, and noise in your communication and the danger of being over-dramatic. Be extra cautious in your handling of your professional life and relationships at work.

 Between November 16 and December 6, Mercury retrogrades in Sagittarius and in Scorpio, your sign. In the first week or two, be aware that Mercury is traveling in your house of finance. Misunderstandings can be expensive. So be extra careful with quotes, financial agreements, and bank statements. Since the end of the retro takes place in your own sign, make sure to be extra conservative with how you present yourself to the world, your outfits, and your health.

SCORPIO

Unpredictable Journey

In 2010, Uranus, the planet of chaos, unpredictability, and revolutions, moved into Aries, which rules your house of health, work, and diet. It meant you had to deal with strange unexpected situations at work or with employees. In addition, your routine went up-side-down. Someone moved into your life who created a great deal of chaos. In addition, you might have had strange ailments or physical problems that were hard to diagnose and disappeared as fast as they arrived. But this is over. From May 2018, Uranus moves into Taurus, which is very personal since it is your opposite sign. Uranus will travel in your house of relationships, marriage, justice, and enemies until 2026. Along with Uranus, a horde of flaky, freedom-loving, crazy, original, and charismatic people will come into your life. It can also make you very funny but create situations where you will act like a rebel without a cause.

If you are in a relationship (personal or business partnership), you might feel the boat is shaking a bit between May and August as Uranus adjusts to his new host. If you don't have a partner, well, Uranus coming into your house of relationships for the first time in 84 years might disrupt whatever was blocking you from having a partner. Maybe Uranus will give you the freedom you need from the freedom that chained you. I know, it sounds crazy, but better get used to this kind of idiocy.

Uranus is freedom, innovation, revolution, and is nicknamed "the joker". When Uranus enters your house of relationships, he can bring these kinds of energies into your partnerships. Humor, freedom, originality, and rejuvenation are crucial to add into your relationships to prevent them from falling apart. Uranus can also bring new exciting and quirky people into your life in general and not only as potential business or love partners. What can I say? you are an intuitive sign and you will have to sift between the crazy and the brilliant, between the disruptive and the exciting. I hope...

 ## Mars Retrograde

This year you are lucky, as Mars will be in your sign! Between December 9, 2017 and Jan 26, 2018, you will host your ruler. It is a time when you will feel like a bundle of energy: powerful, resourceful, and commanding. Mars can make you very passionate and give you the confidence to pursue your goals. However, be careful of accidents, over-aggressive behavior, and impulsiveness.

Mars is the planet of action, passion, and movement. It is your nuclear reactor. It is your solar panel and battery. It is also the planet ruling seeds and vegetation. Since not all of us are farmers, it translates to whatever projects, creations, and enterprises we plan and sow in our lives. When Mars is retro-

SCORPIO ♏

grading (June 26 to August 27) these aspects of life don't work so well. Metaphorically speaking, these fields we tend don't yield good crops. That does not mean nothing will happen. Sometime it is actually good to walk backward. Think of the reverse gear in your car. Where would you be without it? How would you ever be able to park or adjust your position?

During Mars retrograde, you can revisit old projects, make peace, reconnect to past brothers- and sisters-in-arms, reexamine your sexuality and passion, as well as undergo a great deal of healing. As is the rule with all retrograde planets, during the retro period it is safe to engage in any activity that has the prefix *re* – redo, revert, reject, etc. However, it is not recommended to buy big machinery (cars, appliances) or start a war or a lawsuit (whoever shoots first loses). It is not a good time to start a sexual relationship or launch a big project. Not the best for surgery (unless absolutely needed). Try not to be reactive or overly self-protective, especially during Mercury retro that overlaps Mars retro between July 26 and August 18.

Mars retrogrades in Aquarius between June 26 and August 13. That would fall in your house of family and home. If you are a homeowner, make sure you have fire/earthquake insurance. This retrograde can also mean some unnecessary conflicts and aggression with family members. Family members could go through some difficulties.

Between August 13 and August 27, Mars retrogrades in Capricorn. This falls in your house of communication, business, and relatives. It is a good time to review and change the way you

♏ SCORPIO

market yourself or your projects, but be careful of sibling rivalry and conflicts with relatives.

In September, once Mars goes direct, a great deal of projects that were held back can start flowing better. It will be an especially good time to heal relationships with relatives and neighbors, sign contracts, and start new endeavors.

Venus: Money and Love

Venus is the ruler of comfort, luxury, finance, talents, values, art, and relationships. She is also associated with Maat, the goddess of justice and law.

Venus works in beauty cycles: the more you love yourself, the more you believe in yourself. The better your self-image, the more you connect to your talents. The more you develop and invest in your talent, the more money you can make. Venus message is: love yourself and money will follow. Some, however, think that the more money they make, the more they would love themselves and that is a mistake. This year during Venus retrograde (October 6 – November 16), you will be able to change your attitude and fix your relationship to money.

This year Venus will retrograde between October 6 and November 16. First, Venus retrogrades in Scorpio (October 6-31), and then she will retrograde in Libra (October 31 – Nov 16).

SCORPIO ♏

When Venus is retrograding in your sign (October 6 – 31), she can affect how people see you, how you relate to others, as well as create financial setbacks. In general, avoid forming any partnerships and, if possible, don't make big investments or purchases. Venus is retrograding in your first house, the house of your self-image and body. Watch your thyroid, neck, throat, and ovaries.

From Oct 31 to November 16, Venus is retrograding in your house of past lives. It can reconnect you to talents, skills, and people you might have known in previous lives. But sometimes it can also cause relapses into old habits, addictions, or patterns.

Venus retro can also show you who your true allies and real enemies are. Since Venus also rules value, it is a good time to review and change your attitudes, aspirations, and values.

Venus retro is actually a great time to buy second hand goods. It is also a good time to sell things you don't need. However, if you have secret love affairs, this is the time most of them are discovered.

Since Venus is retrograding in your sign, it will spend a great deal of time with you, which is great! Venus is in your sign between September 9 and October 31, and again from December 2,

♏ SCORPIO

2018 until Jan 7, 2019, making you far more attractive to others. It is a great time for romance, making money, and connecting to your artistic side (just watch the retro periods). This is a good time for you to rebrand yourself, dress differently, change your hair, and get some new clothes. Not a bad time to indulge and pamper yourself (as long as it is healthy and does not harm you or anyone else).

Conclusion:

2018 is the year where you can write your great novel, learn how to market yourself, communicate better, as well as possibly open up to new businesses and contracts. Both Venus and Jupiter will be in your sign, and the combination results in a great deal of opportunities and flow. Make the most of this year as many doors are opening for you.

SCORPIO ♏

23RD NOVEMBER – 21ST DECEMBER

SAGITTARIUS

I see my light come shinin' from the west unto the east, any day now, I shall be released. *

key phrase
I see: prophecy

element
Mutable (changeable) fire

planet
Jupiter

day
Thursday

incentive
Embers and torch

body parts
Liver, thighs and hips

color
Blue

stone
Turquoise

---

* Bob Dylan, 1967.

SAGITTARIUS

It wasn't easy. I know. We were all with you, seeing our Sagittarius lighthouses turning dark from the end of 2014 until the end of 2017. But you are the beacon of light and hope. You are the sign of optimism. For crying out loud, look at your neighbors. On one side you have Scorpio, the sign of death, and on the other side, Capricorn, the sign of karma. No wonder you are the sign of hope. Without it, you would never survive! But you have to admit, with all that darkness in the last three years, you grew like never before.

The reason for all the hardships is that, since the end of 2014, Saturn, the lord karma, the teacher of harsh lessons, traveled in your sign. This transit takes place every 30 years, which means that between 1986 and 1989 you experienced similar challenges. It was a spiritual workout, and now you are wiser, stronger, and better than you ever were before. You cannot compare yourself to who you were three years ago. Yes, you might have scars and some traumas, but you are now ready to conquer the world. If you look deeply, you will see that even though it was hard (and thank Goddess it's over), you would not want to erase these years. You know it was worth it. While, right now, you might be shaking your head saying, "No, it wasn't", in a few years, once the wounds are healed, you will thank Saturn for his visit to your sign.

Now that Saturn has left, you can return to the usual fun-loving happy-go-lucky self we love you so much for. Your life will become easier in many ways. It will be especially bright after November 7, 2018, once Jupiter, your planet, moves into your sign and brings in the abundance, luck, and fortune he

SAGITTARIUS ♐

represents. However, one cannot get rid of the grand teacher so easily. In December, 2017, Saturn moved into your house of money, talents, and self-worth. For the next few years you have to buckle up and focus on your talents, finances, and values. Your worth is your talents and your ability to mine them and translate them into income and prosperity. In the next few years, you will be asked to invest time, energy, and faith in your talents. It is time to translate your inner wealth to outer wealth. It might get tight with money, and maybe you will even change the way you make money, but it is all an investment for a more prosperous future.

 With Saturn's strict, stark, and serious nature, Jupiter, your ruler, comes with some good news. Last year, Jupiter was helping you connect to groups, clubs, people, and new friends. You became a connector and connected others. If you worked in an organization or a corporation, you might have managed to climb up the ladder or at least get a better offer from a more suitable and compatible organization. From mid-October, 2017, Jupiter has moved into your house of letting go, mysticism, and past lives. This is a great time to reconnect to skills and talents from previous lives as well as soul-mates and members of your soul-cluster. Jupiter in your house of empathy will make you very sensitive to the point of being a psychic, a mystic, and a medium. Just be careful not to lose yourself in other people's pain and suffering. If you always wanted to join a cause, an NGO, or a nonprofit, this is the year to connect to global action and elevate the suffering of fellow sentient beings.

 SAGITTARIUS

But like I promised, from the second of November, Jupiter will move into your sign and bless you on all levels for 12 months. A lot to look forward to!

 ## The 5 Eclipses – Your Emotional Landscape

As we saw earlier, eclipses quicken processes and push events towards completion. 2018 is a year that will make you feel life is moving faster. You can expect more synchronicities and accelerated stories woven around you.

The eclipses this year, as they were in 2017, are in Leo and Aquarius and these signs vibe very well with your core. You are a Fire Bender, like Leo, and fire needs air, which is Aquarius' element. This means that around the eclipses, things go into turbo mode. Remember the Radiohead song "Karma Police". Karma is real. It has a police force that can stop people who drive too fast and, in your case, ride horses too wildly.

 The lunar eclipse on January 31 is in Leo/Aquarius. These signs rule your houses of travel and communication respectively. This eclipse can create issues in contracts, with your relatives, with in-laws, or with foreigners. It is a good time to complete a study or publish something.

 The solar eclipse on February 15 is focused in the house of communication, writing, and relatives. Since it is the Chinese New Year, it could mean that the next year will be focused around

SAGITTARIUS ♐

study, writing, creating new businesses, and marketing your-self.

The solar eclipse on July 13 is much more emotional as it is happening in Cancer and takes place in your house of sexuality, death, and transformation. Yes, it does not sound very good. Be extra careful in July. It can get dangerous. The eclipse can introduce a great new passion that can be ill-fated. Pace yourself and slow down.

The lunar eclipse on July 27 represents a pull and push between lies and truth, putting your deep sense of authenticity to the test. You will be asked to "walk the talk". Stay true to your inner ethics and morality. It is the biblical celebration of love. Maybe you will find a way to teach or learn abroad. Maybe you will find exotic love with a foreigner or in a different country.

The solar eclipse of August 11 is activating your house of education and travel. It might ignite a journey to a country you have never been to before, find an in-law you really like (or really hate), and some work with multi-national corporations. It might trigger an interest in some new field of study.

 SAGITTARIUS

Mercury Retrograde – Mental Landscape

During Mercury retrograde, it is not recommended to start new long-term projects, sign documents, make large purchases, get married, publish, start marketing campaigns, or release new products. Communications of all sorts are slower and filled with glitches and challenges. Computers crash, stock markets turn volatile, flights are delayed, traffic is worse than usual, accidents occur more often, and Murphy's Law takes hold of our lives. For example, the infamous Flash Crash of May 6, 2010, took place during Mercury retrograde in Taurus (the sign of money and the stock market).

If you must start a new project, be as mindful as you can. Pay attention to small details and read in-between the lines if you must sign a document. Rewrite your emails, edit your texts, and think before you speak. In fact, it is better if you spend more time listening than talking. Life does not come to a halt during Mercury retrograde. You can still achieve a great deal. Mercury retro is like going on a vacation while it is raining. It is still possible but not much fun. However, it is a great time to edit, redo, reexamine yourself and your path, revisit old projects, and find lost objects. It is said that there are more coincidences and more synchronicities when Mercury is retrograding. Try to focus on activities that have the prefix re – reevaluate, reedit, redo, reexamine, reconnect, regenerate, revisit, re-imagine, etc.

SAGITTARIUS ♐

This year Mercury is retrograding in fire signs, which is actually good for you since you, too, are a firecracker. However, pay attention to the last retro which falls in your sign and can cause health issues as well as more acute miscommunications.

 Between March 22 and April 15, Mercury retrogrades in Aries, which rules your house of love, children, sports, and creativity. It can resurrect ex-lovers from the tomb. Be careful not to fall prey to zombie love. It is a time to visit old creative projects but not to publish or release them. There could be some issues and misunderstandings with children.

 Between July 26 and August 18, Mercury retrogrades in Leo, the sign that rules your house of travel. Be extra careful with visas, flight schedules, and how you deal with foreigners. It is a bad time to publish. Be careful of your zealot side and avoid being preachy. It is not good to start a new study or pick a fight with a teacher or an in-law.

 Between November 16 and December 6, Mercury is retrograding in Sagittarius and Scorpio. This can cause health issues. So please boost your immune system, especially if you plan to travel. Since it is happening in your sign, it can cause you mishaps and strange unfortunate events, especially around your birthday. And yes, if you want to get some birthday gifts, remind people when your birthday is because they might forget.

♐ SAGITTARIUS

Unpredictable Journey

In 2010 Uranus, the planet of chaos, unpredictability, and revolutions, moved into Aries. This transit caused some revolutions in your house of love, sports, children, and happiness. It shuffled the cards and forced you to make changes in many aspects of your life. Since Aries is a fellow Fire Bender, it actually helped you find freedom in love, sports, and recreation.

From May 2018, Uranus is moving into Taurus which rules your house of work and health. This presents some unpredictability around your workplace, employees, diet, health, and schedule. Maybe even your pets will act crazy and, if you plan to get a pet, I can assure you it will be highly intelligent, super funny but rebellious, and hard to tame.

Uranus navigates Taurus until 2026. It is a great time to change your work schedule and adjust your diet so it serves you better. Since Uranus in unpredictable, rebellious, and somewhat crazy, that kind of energy is entering your workspace. Uranus is also a call for freedom, a cry for humor and originality, and these things, too, are charging like a raging bull into your work life. It might manifest as a new co-worker that causes revolutions, and it might mean that you yourself become that person. Uranus is also associated with technology, innovation, computers, social media, and originality. Try to ensure that all these aspects are implemented in your work before May. So once Uranus comes into Taurus, it has

SAGITTARIUS ♐

the reception it needs to help you. Be ready for a revolution at work!

Uranus in your house of health can cause unpredictable hard-to-diagnose health issues. The best approach is holistic and preventive medicine. Make sure you juice, improve your diet, cut meat consumption, and exercise regularly.

Mars Retrograde

This year you are lucky, as Mars will be in your sign! Between Jan 26 and March 17, you will host the god of war. That gives you a rare opportunity to hear what the great mythologist, Joseph Campbell, named the "call to adventure". It is your "burning bush" moment, where you will feel an urge to get up and conquer something new. You will feel an inner or outer call to action. When Mars is in your sign, you will feel energized, more attractive, commanding, and sexual. You will feel connected to your passion and drive. However, be careful of accidents, over-aggressive behavior, and impulsiveness.

Mars is the planet of action, passion, and movement. It is your nuclear reactor. It is your solar panel and battery. It is also the planet ruling seeds and vegetation. Since not all of us are farmers, it translates to whatever projects, creations, and enterprises we plan and sow in our lives.

When Mars is retrograding (June 26 to August 27), these aspects of life don't work so well. Metaphorically speaking,

SAGITTARIUS

these fields we tend don't yield good crops. That does not mean nothing will happen. Sometimes it is actually good to walk backwards. Think of the reverse gear in your car. Where would you be without it? How would you ever be able to park or adjust your position?

During Mars retrograde, you can revisit old projects, make peace, reconnect to past brothers- and sisters-in-arms, reexamine your sexuality and passion, as well as undergo a great deal of healing. However, it is not recommended to buy big machinery (cars, appliances) or start a war or a lawsuit (whoever shoots first loses). It is not a good time to start a sexual relationship or launch a big project. Not the best for surgery (unless absolutely needed). Try not to be reactive or overly self-protective, especially during Mercury retro that overlaps Mars retro between July 26 and August 18.

 Mars retrogrades in Aquarius June 26 until August 13. This transit takes place in your house of siblings, communication, businesses, and contracts. All these aspects can feel stuck, annoying, or frustrating. The retrograde period is not a good time for investments or for starting new financial projects as it can lead to arguments, breakups, and unnecessary wars.

 Between August 13 and August 27, Mars is retrograding in Capricorn. This will take place in your house of finance and money. Old talents may return and demand action and attention. But this retrograde can also be expensive as unforeseen spending might force you to dive into savings.

SAGITTARIUS

However, from September, once Mars goes direct, a great deal of projects that were held back can start flowing better. Mars can return some of your lost money or connect you to new sources of income.

 ## Venus: Money and Love

Venus is the ruler of comfort, luxury, finance, talents, values, art, and relationships. She is also associated with Maat, the goddess of justice and law.

Venus works in beauty cycles: the more you love yourself, the more you believe in yourself. The better your self-image, the more you connect to your talents. The more you develop and invest in your talent, the more money you can make. Venus message is: love yourself and money will follow. Some, however, think that the more money they make the more they would love themselves and that is a mistake. This year during Venus retrograde (October 6 – November 16), you will be able to change your attitude and fix your relationship to money.

This year Venus retrogrades between October 6 and November 16. First, Venus retrogrades in Scorpio (October 6-31), and then she will retrograde in Libra (October 31 – Nov 16).

 When Venus is retrograding in Scorpio, it can affect your finances, your investments, and your passion. In general, avoid forming any partnerships and, if possible, don't make big in-

 SAGITTARIUS

vestments or purchases. Venus is retrograding in your house of letting go, hospitals, retreat, and mysticism. Maybe an artistic skill or a relationship from a past lifetime returns to you.

But be extra careful about not falling prey to old addictions. When Venus retrogrades in Libra, she can create challenges with corporations and government. This could lead to misunderstanding and reevaluation of your social circles.

Since Venus also rules value, Venus retrograde is a good time to review and change your attitudes, aspirations, and values. Venus retro is actually a great time to buy second hand goods. It is also a good time to sell things you don't need. However, if you have secret love affairs, this is the time most of them are discovered.

Alas, Venus will not retrograde in your sign this year, but no worries, in 2019 you will get your share of Venus' love.

Conclusion:

This year, you are practicing freedom. After three years of harsh lessons, you will be able to gallop in green fields and feel lighter than ever. 2018 offers a great opportunity to find new talents and original ways of making money. It is a time of revolution in your work. Enjoy the magical mystery tour.

SAGITTARIUS ♐

22ND DECEMBER – 19TH JANUARY

CAPRICORN

*Sometimes I wonder who am I? The world seeming to pass me by.**

key phrase
I USE

element
Cardinal earth

planet
Saturn, the lord of karma and understanding

day
Saturday

incentive
Business plan

body parts
Skin, teeth, skeleton, knees

color
Indigo

stone
Garnet, black onyx, hematite

---

* Lou Reed, 2003.

 CAPRICORN

 In the last few years, Saturn, your ruler, was in the house of letting go. You were asked to do something you didn't feel comfortable doing, and that is to throw things away, to surrender, and to let go of people, attitudes, objects, and habits. Capricorn is the sign that can find a use for everything under the sun. You are the MacGyver of the zodiac. After all, your key word is "I use". You can find something useful in any object, person, or situation, but as Saturn, the lord of karma and provider of tough lessons, was in your house of abandonment and separation, he forced you to visit the dumpster more often than you would have liked.

Saturn is your planet and therefore has a special relationship with you. He is like your father who is also the CEO of the zodiac. He loves you more than the other signs, but he also expects much more from you. For the last few years, Saturn was making you feel trapped, confined, jailed, and stuck. In other words, Saturn was in your house of pain and the only way to elevate the pain was to let go, surrender, and move on. You might have felt betrayed, abandoned, and all alone on the battlefield. In many ways, this is an accurate description of life since the end of 2014. But it is not all darkness and gloom. The house of letting go is also the house of mysticism and empathy. You were given a chance to strip off your shell and find your true spiritual core. You felt like a car in the car wash. The universe scrubbed you, and now you are sparkling clean, ready for a new beginning. The last time this happened was 1987–1990. In that period, you crafted an identity. In the last three years, you let go of that image of yourself, and now you are free to be whomever you wish to become.

CAPRICORN

When Saturn moves into a sign, it is usually not good news to that sign, as no one really wants to host the stern master. But since Capricorn is governed by Saturn, it means that you are getting the personal trainer you always dreamt about: a harsh, no nonsense kind of guy that gets results. In the next few years, you have a rare chance of reinventing, rebranding, and sculpting a new self. This is the time you can get the body you always wished for, repair your public image, change your style, outfits, hair, and even location. Saturn affords you the ability once in 30 years to become the best version of yourself. It demands discipline, persistence, focus, and a plan, but you can make miracle happen.

This year, you will have one question in mind: who am I? Usually, you are not concerned with such existential questions but, just like Alice was asked who she was by the caterpillar, you too will have to come up with an answer in order to make it into your wonderland. And even though Capricorn can be pessimistic, I can assure you that the universe will help you come up with an answer. For all questions, asked in the right time, are answered by time. And Saturn, Chronos, the ancient Greek Lord of Time, is your father. He will give you the keys to his Cadillac.

Be careful not to be too hard on yourself and too demanding. The change will take time, but

♑ CAPRICORN

it's okay as you are the sign of patience. If you can sit down and imagine where you want to be, who you want to be, and with whom you want to be, in the next three years, you can make it happen. Remember, the focus this year is your identity on all levels: physical, spiritual, financial, emotional, and mental.

 With Saturn's strict, stark, and serious nature, Jupiter comes with some good news. Last year, Jupiter was in your house of career, opening doors and presenting opportunities to expand and cement your career. It was a good time to work with father figures and bosses as well as to put down seeds that could positively transform your social status and recognition in your career. From mid-October 2017, Jupiter moved into your house of friends, corporations, community, and altruism. If you are working in a company, you can expect a raise or promotion. Something wonderful is happening with your friends and contacts. You will feel open to new friendships as well as to joining new clubs, organizations, and perhaps an offer from a new company. This year also presents a good time for making wishes come true. Pay extra attention to your New Year's resolution for it actually might come true.

From the second week of November, Jupiter, the benevolent planet and giver of gifts, will move into your house of letting go, and he will help you fine-tune all the lessons of the year as well as connect you to your spiritual and mystical side. For the 12 months that follow November 2018, you will feel your psychic abilities, intuition, and dream life enhanced and made practical.

CAPRICORN

The 5 Eclipses –
Your Emotional Landscape

Eclipses quicken processes and push events towards completion. 2018 is a year that will make you feel life is moving faster. You can expect more synchronicities and accelerated stories woven around you. This year you are letting go of the past completely, no turning back. After all, the year started on a full moon in your sign and the full moon represents endings.

The eclipses this year are in the Leo/Aquarius axis, which is not comfortable to for you. Their element is fire and air, while you are an Earth Bender. You like to take your time and they don't believe time is real. You will feel pushed into doing things you might not be ready to do. Think twice before acting and try to remain calm.

 The lunar eclipse on January 31 places the moon in your house of sexuality and passion, while the sun will be in your house of finance and self-worth. Are you passionate about what you do for a living? Maybe the eclipse can shine a new talent or give you the confidence to change the way you make money. It can also pit your earning against your partner's income.

 The solar eclipse on February 15, the Chinese New Year, is focused in the house of money, talents, and self-worth. This means that the year can be colored by questions about your income and how authentic you are in your professional life. Re-

♑ CAPRICORN

member, the eclipses this year are focused on passion and money, talents, and your drive. Since you are trying to re-brand yourself and you are a practical sign, much of the reinvention has to be around your income and earning potential.

 The solar eclipse on July 13 is far easier for you to handle as it is in Cancer, a water sign that can sprinkle some compassion into your Capricorn garden. Cancer is your opposite sign and therefore falls in your house of relationships and marriage. Maybe a new partner in life or work appears. Make sure to spend time near water.

 The lunar eclipse on July 27 is the biblical celebration of love. It is a time when things around finance, passion, death, and transformation are quickened and come to some resolution. Again, you might find a conflict between your desires and your partner's needs, especially concerning money and finances. It is a time to be generous but also to be true to your values.

The solar eclipse of August 11 is once again in your house of sexuality, investment, production, and joint artistic and financial affairs. It is a good time to collaborate with other people and incorporate their talents with yours.

CAPRICORN ♑

Mercury Retrograde – Mental Landscape

During Mercury retrograde, it is not recommended to start new long-term projects, sign documents, make large purchases, get married, publish, start marketing campaigns, or release new products. Communications of all sorts are slower and filled with glitches and challenges. Computers crash, stock markets turn volatile, flights are delayed, traffic is worse than usual, accidents occur more often, and Murphy's Law takes hold of our lives. For example, the infamous Flash Crash of May 6, 2010, took place during Mercury retrograde in Taurus (the sign of money and the stock market).

If you must start a new project, be as mindful as you can. Pay attention to small details and read in-between the lines if you must sign a document. Rewrite your emails, edit your texts and think before you speak. In fact, it is better if you spend more time listening than talking. Life does not come to a halt during Mercury retrograde. You can still achieve a great deal. Mercury retro is like going on a vacation while it is raining. It is still possible but not much fun. However, it is a great time to edit, redo, reexamine yourself and your path, revisit old projects, and find lost objects. It is said that there are more coincidences and more synchronicities when Mercury is retrograding. Try to focus on activities that have the prefix re – reevaluate, reedit, redo, reexamine, reconnect, regenerate, revisit, re-imagine, etc.

♑ CAPRICORN

This year, Mercury is retrograding in fire signs which, as we saw with the eclipses, is not easy for you. Capricorn is structured and patient, you are like the CEO who wants the operations to run smoothly, but during Mercury retrograde, this is not easy to accomplish.

Between March 22 and April 15, Mercury is retrograde in Aries. Aries has never been an easy sign for you. It is a childish and impulsive sign, while you are cautious and mature. This Mercury retrograde is in your house of home and family. Avoid any purchases for the home or of homes and real-estate. There might be some misunderstandings with family members.

Between July 26 and August 18, Mercury retrogrades in Leo, the sign that is in your house of death, inheritance, transformation, sexuality, and passion. This can bring a great deal of magic into your life. Maybe even an ability to dream about or communicate with someone you lost. Ex-lovers or intimate partners might come back into your life. Not a good time for investments and there might be some snags with payments or finances.

Between November 16 and December 6, Mercury is retrograding in Sagittarius and Scorpio. There can be some issues and challenges within your company or with friends. Since it also falls in your house of letting go, take this period of time to peel off the last few layers or obstacles that hold you back.

CAPRICORN

Unpredictable Journey

In 2010, Uranus, the planet of chaos, unpredictability, and revolutions, moved into Aries. For the last 7 years, Uranus was in your house of home and family. Uranus was causing a great deal of unpredictable and sometime disturbing events relating to family members and properties. Not good or bad, just weird. It is never easy for you to deal with Uranus which represents rebellion with tradition. Since in the last 7 years as Uranus was in Aries, the sign of war, you had some family feuds and other kinds of aggression with people you consider family.

On May 2018, Uranus moves in Taurus, a fellow earth sign, and will be there until 2026. This means you might get a good push forward, especially if you are open to connecting to technology and younger, innovative people. There is a chance that it will rejuvenate and invigorate you.

Uranus in Taurus activates your house of children, happiness, and love. If you have children, they might become more rebellious in the next few years. It can also attract crazy, charismatic, and ingenious lovers, who, in addition, can be flaky and freedom loving. Uranus represents freedom and when it is in your house of love, well, it means free love. Since that house is also the house of creativity and children of the mind, you might bring forth some brilliant and innovative creative projects especially related to technology, patents, innovation, and e-commerce.

 CAPRICORN

It is a great year to start a new hobby or sport that has to do with the outdoors and that can propel you to connect to new groups of people, who, if not younger than you, then are at least young in their attitudes and behaviors. Yes, 2018 is both frightening and exciting at the same time. Just try to have fun!

Mars Retrograde

Mars is the planet of action, passion, and movement. It is your nuclear reactor. It is your solar panel and battery. It is also the planet ruling seeds and vegetation. Since not all of us are farmers, it translates to whatever projects, creations, and enterprises we plan and sow in our lives.

Mars has a special connection to you. When Mars is in Capricorn, it is considered exalted, meaning it can express its full potential. Under your sign, Mars transforms into a disciplined special operations soldier. This year, you are lucky to host Mars in your sign between March 17 and May 16 and again between August 13 and September 11. That gives you a rare opportunity to hear what the great mythologist, Joseph Campbell, named the "call to adventure". It is your "burning bush" moment, where you will feel an urge to get up and conquer something new. You will feel an inner or outer call to action. When Mars is in your sign, you will feel energized, more attractive and sexual, and more connected to your passion and drive. Be careful not to be too impulsive (yes, it can even

happen to you). You will become Muhamad Ali, who was a fellow Capricorn, and knock your enemies out.

 When Mars is retrograding (June 26 to August 27), life slows down a bit and can create un-necessary wars. Be extra careful when Mars retrogrades in your sign between August 13 and 27. Mars retrograde does not mean nothing will happen. Sometimes it is actually good to walk backwards. Think of the reverse gear in your car. Where would you be without it? How would you ever be able to park or adjust your position?

During Mars retrograde, you can revisit old projects, make peace, reconnect to past brothers- and sisters-in-arms, reexamine your sexuality and passion, as well as undergo a great deal of healing. However, it is not recommended to buy big machinery (cars, appliances) or start a war or a lawsuit (whoever shoots first loses). It is not a good time to start a sexual relationship or launch a big project. Not the best for surgery (unless absolutely needed). Try not to be reactive or overly self-protective, especially during Mercury retro that overlaps Mars retro between July 26 and August 18.

 Mars retrogrades in Aquarius from June 26 until August 13. This takes place in your house of money, talents, and self-worth. Try not to spend money or go on shopping therapy sprees. You might feel swings from feeling too good to too bad about yourself. There could be some money or investments coming back to you at this time.

VƷ CAPRICORN

When Mars retrogrades in Capricorn, between August 13 and August 27, it will be more dangerous to your body and health. So please be careful of injuries or of over-training. Burnouts, stress, and anxiety can manifest. So please pace yourself. However, from September, once Mars goes direct, a great deal of projects that were held back can start flowing better. That would be a good time to

assert yourself, ask for a raise, start a new project, and assume a position of leadership.

Venus: Money and Love

2018 begins with a blessing. From Dec 25, 2017 to January 18, 2018, Venus is in your sign. It is a great time for romance, making money, and connecting to your artistic side. This is a good time for you to rebrand yourself, dress differently, change your hair, and get some new clothes. Not a bad time to indulge and pamper yourself (as long as it is healthy and does not harm you or anyone else).

Venus works in beauty cycles: the more you love yourself, the more you believe in yourself. The better your self-image, the more you connect to your talents. The more you develop

CAPRICORN ♑

and invest in your talent, the more money you can make. Venus message is: love yourself and money will follow. Some, however, think that the more money they make, the more they would love themselves and that is a mistake. This year during Venus retrograde (October 6 – November 16), you will be able to change your attitude and fix your relationship to money.

This year, Venus will retrograde between October 6 and November 16. First, Venus retrogrades in Scorpio from October 6 to 31, and then it retrogrades in Libra, between October 31 and Nov 16. When Venus is retrograding in Scorpio, she can affect your finances, investments, and passion. In general, avoid forming any partnerships and, if possible, don't make big investments or purchases. Be extra careful in your dealings with your friends and co-workers as Venus falls in your house of community. Venus retrograde could also mean a friend you have not seen in years or a company you used to work with will come back into your life. But pay attention to extra fees, taxes, or permits from government as there could be some issues with red tape. When Venus retrogrades in Libra, she can create challenges but also profound lessons in relationships and partnerships. She can also jeop-

♑ CAPRICORN

ardize your self-worth, self-esteem, and earning potential. Venus falls in your house of career. Therefore, pay extra attention to your dealings with authority figures.

Venus retro can also show you who your true allies and real enemies are. Since Venus also rules value, it is a good time to review and change your attitudes, aspirations, and values. Venus retro is actually a great time to buy second hand goods. It is also a good time to sell things you don't need. However, if you have secret love affairs, this is the time most of them are discovered.

Conclusion:

This is a powerful year for you Capricorns. You are out of jail and trying to discover who you are and what your new self looks like. This is a year you can change everything and rebrand yourself. Look back at what happened between 1990-1993 and you will get clues as to what is expected of you in 2018 and how to become the master that you are.

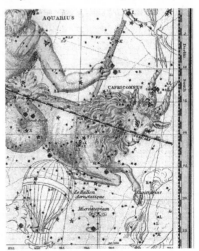

CAPRICORN ♑

21ST JANUARY – 18TH FEBRUARY

AQUARIUS

Let it go, let it go, can't hold it back anymore. *

key phrase
I KNOW

element
Fixed (unchangeable) air

planet
Uranus

day
Saturday

incentive
Friendship

body parts
Ankles, shinbones and circulatory system

color
Violet

stone
Sapphire

* Frozen, 2013.

 AQUARIUS

 Saturn, known in Kabbalah as the recti-fier, the fixer, teaches us with the stick rather than the carrot. In the last few years, Saturn was teaching you the meaning of community and friends. I know what you are thinking. You are the sign of friendships and fraternity. Why should you need to learn what you already know? But every 30 years, you need to reevaluate your place in the world and, from the end of 2014 until end of 2017, Saturn offered you an opportunity to change your clubs, friends, organizations, and company. You were asked to look into your core and see what you truly be-lieve in.

In 2018, Saturn shifts gears and moves into your house of letting go, retreat, and mysticism. It is also called the house of pain and suffering. It does not mean the next few years are going to be hell. This house is not an easy place to walk through, but it gives you the opportunity to peel off what is called in Kabbalah, your Klipoth, your shell, exocarp, your obstacles, and your ego. It already happened between 1990 and1993. You can go back to that period and see what you were asked to let go of. The key word to succeed in the next few years is "surrender". It does not mean you have to give up or feel defeated. It means you have to learn how to flow, surf the waves of synchronici-ties, and relax into the current.

AQUARIUS

Saturn can help you release and cut away things that held you back such as extra weight, substance abuse, dependent relationships, financial hardships, or any other patterns that kept you in a loop. Once Saturn moves into your sign (2020/2021), you will have the opportunity to reinvent yourself. Until then, you are stripping away old habits. You are breaking down the wall, one brick after the other.

It is not all doom and gloom. In fact, many people find a wonderful release during this transit. You will be able to dive into past lifetimes and reconnect to skills, talents, and gifts you possessed in previous lives. Maybe you will even meet soulmates, friends, and fellow soul-tribe members you have not seen for centuries. It is also a good time to volunteer and work with the suffering of others.

 With Saturn's strict, stark, and serious nature, Jupiter comes with some good news. Last year, Jupiter was in your house of travel and education. It was helping you connect to your truth and creed. Jupiter opened doors that relate to foreign cultures and higher education. From mid-October, 2017, Jupiter moved into your house of career. This is very good news on the professional level. There could be promotion, raise, new career opportunities, and a chance to become a leader in your workspace. It is also a good time to heal relationships with father figures, your own father, or bosses.

From the second week of November, Jupiter, the giver of gifts, will open doors for you in your social circles, companies, and corporations. You will be able to easily climb the corporate ladder or make new friends, join new clubs and

AQUARIUS

groups, and reconnect to the most important thing for an Aquarius: community.

The 5 Eclipses –
Your Emotional Landscape

Eclipses quicken processes and push events towards completion. 2018 is a year that will make you feel life is moving faster. You can expect more synchronicities and accelerated stories woven around you. Last year, the eclipse axis shifted into your sign as well as into your opposite sign, Leo. Look back to February and August of 2017. You must have experienced many shifts and changes. The trend continues this year and the months to watch are January, February, July, and August. The last time the eclipses were in Aquarius and Leo was 1999 and 1980. Try to identify what significant events took place then, as an echo or a reverberation of these situations is coming back this year.

The lunar eclipse on January 31 is in Leo/Aquarius. This lunar eclipse pits your own needs against your partner's needs. It will be "me versus you" or "I versus us". The moon will be in the house of partners (in life and in work), and the sun, your ego, will be in the house of "me, myself and I". During this time, partners can easily transform into enemies. This eclipse can also affect your health and emotional state. The more connected you are to your feelings, the less likely you are to get sick.

The solar eclipse on February 15 falls on the Chinese New Year. The Chinese New Year always takes place on the new

AQUARIUS

moon in Aquarius. Yes! You are the initiator of the Chinese Zodiac. It is a great honor. It means that this year is focused on your body, health, and identity. Again, you are asked to peel off layers in order to find your true core. Do something nice for yourself today. Emphasize yourself. Give yourself a gift. It is your lunar birthday eclipse.

The solar eclipse on July 13 can be very emotional as it takes place in Cancer, which is not a comfortable sign for you. Yes, you are the water bearer but you are also an Air Bender and you would rather invent a way to move water around than be forced to carry the water buckets yourself. A Cancer eclipse is a great deal of water to carry. The eclipse falls in your house of health, diet, pets, and work. There could be some emotional upset or confusion in your workspace or with employees. Watch your digestive system and stomach. In general, it is a good time for a cleanse or a detox.

The lunar eclipse on July 27 falls on the biblical day of love and takes place in your house of relationship. Again, you might feel a push and pull between your needs and those of your partner. Watch out for enemies and lawsuits as the eclipse is happening while Mars is retrograding. On a more positive note, this eclipse can bring a new love into your life.

The solar eclipse of August 11 is in your house of marriage, partners, and justice. This eclipse can bring a new collaboration or even a new partner in work or in life.

AQUARIUS

Mercury Retrograde – Mental Landscape

During Mercury retrograde, it is not recommended to start new long-term projects, sign documents, make large purchases, get married, publish, start marketing campaigns, or release new products. Communications of all sorts are slower and filled with glitches and challenges. Computers crash, stock markets turn volatile, flights are delayed, traffic is worse than usual, accidents occur more often, and Murphy's Law takes hold of our lives. For example, the infamous Flash Crash of May 6, 2010, took place during Mercury retrograde in Taurus (the sign of money and the stock market).

If you must start a new project, be as mindful as you can. Pay attention to small details and read in-between the lines if you must sign a document. Rewrite your emails, edit your texts and think before you speak. In fact, it is better if you spend more time listening than talking. Life does not come to a halt during Mercury retrograde. You can still achieve a great deal. Mercury retro is like going on a vacation while it is raining. It is still possible but not much fun. However, it is a great time to edit, redo, reexamine yourself and your path, revisit old projects, and find lost objects. It is said that there are more coincidences and more

AQUARIUS ♒

synchronicities when Mercury is retrograding. Try to focus on activities that have the prefix re – reevaluate, reedit, redo, re-examine, reconnect, regenerate, revisit, re-imagine, etc.

As an Air Bender, the Mercury retrogrades this year will be easier for you to handle. You are an air sign and the retrogrades take place in fire signs. The alchemy is flowing for you.

 Between March 22 and April 15, Mercury retrogrades in Aries. This Mercury retrograde falls in your house of communication. Since Aries is a blunt and aggressive sign, you might get into conflict because of what you said (or didn't say). Be careful not to be snappy or cut people off. This is a period when small misunderstandings can get out of control.

 Between July 26 and August 18, Mercury retrogrades in Leo, your opposite sign. This could manifest as misunderstandings with your business partners or in love relationships. Since it is in Leo, a very dramatic sign, comedy can transform into tragedy very fast. Avoid roaring and exercise patience with your contractual relations and significant others.

 The last retrograde takes place between November 16 and December 6. Since this retrograde is happening in Sagittarius and Scorpio, it affects your houses of career and friends. If you are working in an organization, there could be some miscommunication with co-workers, bosses, and authority figures. If you are self-employed or a stay-at-home person, be mindful of governmental bureaucracy, permits, taxes, or miscommunications with friends.

 AQUARIUS

Unpredictable Journey

In 2010, Uranus, your ruler, the planet of chaos, unpredictability, and revolutions, moved into Aries. For the last 7 years, there has been a lot of change, chaos, and unpredictability in your communication, marketing, writing, and connections to relatives. You had to change the way you talk and deliver information. You had to deal with your thought patterns and how you do business. On May 16, 2018, Uranus moves into Taurus, the sign of finances, money, talent, and self-worth.

While Uranus is your planet and therefore has a special connection to you, it is not comfortable for your tribe when he transits through Taurus. Both Aquarius and Taurus (along with Leo and Scorpio) are fixed signs and tend to be fixated and stubborn. This year, it will be good for you to practice being flexible physically (yoga, stretching), emotionally, spiritually, and mentally.

 When Uranus is in Taurus, it falls in your house of home and family and can create a great deal of chaos on the home front. It can also affect mother figures or anyone else in your life that nurtures and heals you. Since the house of home is the foundation of your chart, it means that Uranus is shaking the core of your soul. May, June, and July, as well as August with its eclipse, can feel a bit uncomfortable. As long as you have your community of friends for support and your sense of humor is active, you will be fine and will be able to weather the storm.

AQUARIUS

Uranus in the house of home is not all bad, especially if you can upgrade your living space, move to a modern place, make it more high-tech, and change your neighborhood to a place that has a better sense of community.

 ## Mars Retrograde

This year, Mars will be in your sign between May 16 and August 13 and again between September 11 and November 15. That gives you a rare opportunity to hear what the great mythologist, Joseph Campbell, named the "call to adventure". It is your "burning bush" moment, when you will feel an urge to get up and conquer something new. You will hear an inner or outer call to action. When Mars is in your sign, you will feel energized, attractive, sexual, and deeply connected to your passion and drive. Be careful not to be too impulsive and over-aggressive. It is a time when you can assume a leadership position in your company, organization, or community. Be extra careful when Mars retrogrades in your sign, between June 26 and August 13. This can cause injuries, regrets, and issues with anger, as well as periods of withdrawal and fatigue.

Mars is the planet of action, passion, and movement. It is your nuclear reactor. It is your solar panel and battery. It is also the planet ruling seeds and vegetation. Since not all of us are farmers, it translates to whatever projects, creations, and enterprises we plan and sow in our lives.

However, this year, Mars is retrograding (June 26 to August 27). Metaphorically speaking, the fields we tend don't yield good crops. That does not mean nothing will happen. Sometimes it is actually good to walk backwards. Think of the reverse gear in your car. Where would you be without it? How would you ever be able to park or adjust your position?

During Mars retrograde, you can revisit old projects, make peace, reconnect to past brothers- and sisters-in-arms, reexamine your sexuality and passion, as well as undergo a great deal of healing. However, it is not recommended to buy big machinery (cars, appliances) or start a war or a lawsuit (whoever shoots first loses). It is not a good time to start a sexual relationship or launch a big project. Not the best for surgery (unless absolutely needed). Try not to be reactive or overly self-protective, especially during Mercury retro that overlaps Mars retro between July 26 and August 18.

As I mentioned above, Mars retrogrades in your sign between June 26 and August 13: watch your body and your self-image. There could be some people trying to tarnish your reputation. Be careful of physical injuries and mishaps. Drive slowly! When Mars retrogrades in Capricorn, August 13 to August 27, it joins Saturn in your house of letting go and will ask you to rid yourself of behaviors and habits that might be detrimental to your personality or well-being. It is a good time for a yoga retreat or any other self-induced withdrawal.

In September, once Mars goes direct, you will feel energized and refreshed. Many projects that were held back can start flowing better.

AQUARIUS

Venus: Money and Love

Venus is the ruler of comfort, luxury, finance, talents, values, art, and relationships. She is also associated with Maat, the goddess of justice and law. When Venus is in your sign (Jan 18 to February 10), you appear far more attractive to others. It is a great time for romance, making money, and connecting to your artistic side. This is a good time for you to rebrand yourself, dress differently, change your hair, get some new clothes. Not a bad time to indulge and pamper yourself (as long as it is healthy and does not harm you or anyone else).

Venus works in beauty cycles: the more you love yourself, the more you believe in yourself. The better your self-image, the more you connect to your talents. The more you develop and invest in your talent, the more money you can make. Venus message is: love yourself and money will follow. Some, however, think that the more money they make, the more they would love themselves and that is a mistake. This year during Venus retrograde (October 6 – November 16), you will be able to change your attitude and fix your relationship to money.

 In 2018, Venus will retrograde between October 6 and November 16. First, Venus retrogrades in Scorpio from October 6 to 31, and then she retrogrades in Libra, between October 31 and Nov 16. When Venus is retrograding in Scorpio, she can affect your finance, investments, and pas-

AQUARIUS

sion. In general, avoid forming any partnerships and, if possible, don't make big investments or purchases. Be extra careful in your career and relationships with father figures, bosses, and co-workers. When Venus retrogrades in Libra, she can create challenges but also profound lessons in relationships and partnerships especially with foreigners, in-laws, or people who are involved in your education (teachers, mentors, professors). Venus retro can also jeopardize your self-worth, self-esteem, and earning potential.

Venus retrograde can show you who your true allies and your real enemies are. Since Venus also rules value, it is a good time to review and change your attitudes, aspirations, and values. Venus retro is actually a great time to buy second hand goods. It is also a good time to sell things you don't need. However, if you have secret love affairs, this is the time most of them are discovered.

Conclusion:

I know you know. After all, the key words for your sign are "I know". But what always makes Aquarius ingenious is the fact that they also know that they don't know. This year, you will experience expansion in your career, especially if you manage to identify what you need to cut out of your life. It is a time for a purge and cleanup that can help you get rid of whatever keeps you from enlightenment.

PISCES

*I get high with a little help from my friends.**

key phrase
I IMAGINE

element
Mutable (changeable) water

planet
Neptune, the lord of the oceans

day
Thursday

incentive
Mysticism

body parts
Feet, immune system, lymphatic system

color
Violet-black

stone
Amethyst

---

* The Beatles, 1967.

 PISCES

In the last few years, Saturn, the Lord Karma and deliverer of harsh lessons, was transiting in your house of career and social status. Saturn is associated with professional success and, when it moved to fix your career, it was rather intense for your tribe of dolphins. Saturn was holding the stick rather than the carrot and hit you on the head like a Zen master trying to enlighten a stubborn disciple. It was not easy with your father, bosses, or other authority figures. You experienced pressure and a great deal of frustration in your career. It felt like some roads were blocked, while others were impossible to walk on. But if you were disciplined, had a plan, and managed to carry the extra responsibility, by now your career should be in a better place.

From the last week of 2017, Saturn started its journey in your house of community, friends, and governments. You will find yourself changing your social circles, club associations, and the kind of people you hang out with. Old friends will drift away, making room to new ones. The last time this happened was between 1990 and1993. It will be a good idea to go back to these years and see how you were doing with friends, companies, and organizations at that time and learn from past mistakes.

Usually when Saturn is in the house of friends, it can create situations that force you to reassess your social circles. Maybe you hang out with some people just because you are afraid of being alone? Maybe some of your friends are with you for the wrong reasons? After all, you tend to be very empathic and attract dependent and codependent relationships.

PISCES

Saturn can break the cords with those who hold you back. Saturn will show you who your real friends are and who are just there to use or abuse you. Since Saturn is also working to fix your standing in your community, some of you will experience a change in your company or corporation. Reshuffling in management or change of ownership can make you decide to leave your company and find another place to work.

In addition, Saturn can bring back into your life people who you have not seen in many years or in many lifetimes. Souls that are connected to your spiritual tribe will return. It usually happens through a series of synchronicities and serendipities. It will most likely happen during eclipses (January, February, July, August). Since Saturn is also in your house of government, pay extra attention to permits, governmental red tape, taxes, or any other duties coming from the authorities.

With Saturn's strict, stark, and serious nature, Jupiter comes with a breath of fresh air. Last year, Jupiter was helping you get connected to your sexuality, passion, productions, inheritance, and joint artistic and financial affairs. Jupiter, who loves your sign, gave you the super power of the Lady Death, which is to cut what you don't need, to be a shaman, to connect to the occult and afterlife, as well as to explore your healing and sexual powers. It was a wonderful journey into intimacy and magic.

Since mid-October 2017, Jupiter moved into your house of travel, education, and truth. Jupiter can give you blessings and benevolence if you harken to his message: be authentic, be real to yourself, say yes to every opportunity to travel, espe-

♓ PISCES

cially abroad or for education. This is a great time to study or work with foreigners or in a different country. If you had any issues with in-laws, this a great time to heal and change your relationships with them. In 2018, you will find many opportunities to teach, consult, and share your wisdom. 2018 is the best year for higher-education or learning a new language. Jupiter will also bless publishing, mass media enterprises, marketing, and writing. So we expect to hear about you this year!

From the second week of 2018, Jupiter will move into your house of career for 12 months. Expect a raise, promotion, or clarity in your professional life.

 ## The 5 Eclipses – Your Emotional Landscape

Eclipses quicken processes and push events towards completion. 2018 is a year that will make you feel life is moving faster. You can expect more synchronicities and accelerated stories woven around you. The moon loves you since you are a Water Bender and she can see herself reflected in your watery surfaces. This year, try to work with the cycles of the moon so you can surf its swelling waves: on each new moon start a project; on the full moon, rest; and when the moon is waning, edit or cut things out of the project.

The eclipses this year take place in the Leo/Aquarius axis, which is not easy for you. It is not the best compatibility as water does not mix well with fire (Leo) and air (Aquarius). You will feel as if life is pushing you too hard. Therefore, during the eclipses, try to avoid over-scheduling or over-stretching yourself.

PISCES ♓

The lunar eclipse on January 31 in Leo/Aquarius falls in your houses of letting go and health. Pay extra attention to your immune system and pace yourself in work and in life in general. Planning a ski trip? Well, take it easy with the diamond slopes.

The Chinese New Year solar eclipse that takes place on February 15 is focused on your house of mysticism and past lives. You might reconnect to a talent or to a skill from a previous life. It is a good time to retreat from life for a few days. Rent a cabin somewhere and isolate yourself. It can be an extra-emotional time. So be kind to yourself and do something nice for you.

The solar eclipse on July 13 is far easier to handle as it falls in Cancer, a fellow water sign. It activates your house of love, happiness, children, and creativity. This means you can actually find love, feel childlike and creative. It is a great time to get pregnant or spend time with your children or anyone who brings out your curious, fun-loving, inner child.

The lunar eclipse on July 27, the biblical day of love, might make you feel tired or sick. It can create challenges with co-workers or employees. Please watch your diet around that time and don't overwork or over-book your schedule.

The solar eclipse on August 11 is in your house of work and diet. It could present an opportunity to make the changes you want in those areas.

♓ PISCES

Even though it is Mercury retrograde, this is not a bad time to contemplate a change of direction in your professional life.

☿ Mercury Retrograde – ♃ Mental Landscape

During Mercury retrograde, it is not recommended to start new long-term projects, sign documents, make large purchases, get married, publish, start marketing campaigns, or release new products. Communications of all sorts are slower and filled with glitches and challenges. Computers crash, stock markets turn volatile, flights are delayed, traffic is worse than usual, accidents occur more often, and Murphy's Law takes hold of our lives. For example, the infamous Flash Crash of May 6, 2010, took place during Mercury retrograde in Taurus (the sign of money and the stock market).

If you must start a new project, be as mindful as you can. Pay attention to small details and read in-between the lines if you must sign a document. Rewrite your emails, edit your texts, and think before you speak. In fact, it is better if you spend more time listening than talking. Life does not come to a halt during Mercury retrograde. You can still achieve a great deal. Mercury retro is like going on a vacation while it is raining. It is still possible but not much fun. However, it is a great time to edit, redo, reexamine yourself and your path, revisit old projects, and find lost objects. It is said that there are more coincidences and more synchronicities when Mercury is retrograding. Try to focus on activities that have the prefix re –

PISCES ♓

reevaluate, reedit, redo, reexamine, reconnect, regenerate, revisit, re-imagine, etc.

This year Mercury is retrograding in fire signs, which might be a bit harder for you as you are a water creature. But maybe a bit of fire can ignite you and propel you to move forward.

Mercury retrogrades between March 22 and April 15 in Aries. Aries is not an easy sign for you. You represent empathy and world-peace, while Aries is the ruthless warrior that disrupts these peaceful attempts. This Mercury retrograde takes place in your house of money and self-worth. Please make sure not to spend money or make investments.

Mercury retrogrades between July 26 and August 18 in Leo. This can add pressure in your workplace and cause misunderstanding with co-workers or employees. The retro also falls in your house of health. It is a good time to review and change your diet. Since your pets can be affected by this retrograde, take extra care of your furry friends.

Mercury retrogrades between November 16 and December 6 in Sagittarius and Scorpio. This Mercury can cause miscommunications and glitches in your career and a great deal of discomfort with your bosses or authority figures (including your father). If you plan to travel, make sure all your papers are in order as there could be some glitches while traveling abroad.

 PISCES

Unpredictable Journey

In 2010, Uranus, the planet of chaos, unpredictability, and revolutions, moved into Aries. For 7 years, he was in your house of money, talent, and self-worth, causing radical swings in your financial situation as well as how you perceived yourself. Sometimes you felt like you were the best thing that happened since the Big-Bang, and other times you felt lower than a worm. From May, as Uranus moves away from your house of money, finance will start aligning itself and become more balanced.

When Uranus is in Taurus, it is not too bad for you. You are a water sign, and Taurus is the holy grail that can contain your holy water. Uranus will transit in your house of communication, writing, business, contracts, and relatives until 2026. The joker will pull some jokes on you and you need to learn how to laugh with him. You will find yourself far more witty and funny but also experience bouts of rebellion. Be careful not to destroy things in your life with the way you communicate or through what you write. Be especially careful with your digital writing (social media, web sites).

Relationships with siblings can be a bit bumpy and you do have to watch what you sign as contracts can be broken or changed. Make sure there is a clear exit strategy in documents you sign. However, Uranus can also help you connect to startups, e-commerce, and download a great deal of brilliant ideas. You might think of a patent or at least some in-

PISCES ♓

genious businesses idea. It is as if Uranus can raise your IQ but also cause you to behave like a mad professor.

 ## Mars Retrograde

Mars is the planet of action, passion, and movement. It is your nuclear reactor. It is your solar panel and battery. It is also the planet ruling seeds and vegetation. Since not all of us are farmers, it translates to whatever projects, creations, and enterprises we plant and sow in our lives.

 This year, Mars will be in your sign from November 15 until the end of the year. That gives you a rare opportunity to hear what the great mythologist, Joseph Campbell, named the "call to adventure". It is your "burning bush" moment, when you will feel an urge to get up and conquer something new. You will hear an inner or outer call to action. When Mars is in your sign, you feel energized, attractive, and sexual as well as deeply connected to your passion and drive. Be careful not to be too impulsive and over-aggressive. It is a time when you can assume a leadership position and lead your community.

However, when Mars is retrograding (June 26 to August 27), the aspects of life that are governed by Mars don't work so well. Metaphorically speaking, the fields we tend don't yield good crops. That does not mean nothing will happen. Sometimes it is actually good to walk backwards. Think of the reverse gear in your car. Where would you be without it? How would you ever be able to park or adjust your position?

♓ PISCES

During Mars retrograde, you can revisit old projects, make peace, reconnect to past brothers- and sisters-in-arms, reexamine your sexuality and passion, as well as undergo a great deal of healing. However, it is not recommended to buy big machinery (cars, appliances) or start a war or a lawsuit (whoever shoots first loses). It is not a good time to start a sexual relationship or launch a big project. Not the best for surgery (unless absolutely needed). Try not to be reactive or overly self-protective especially during Mercury retro that overlaps Mars retro between July 26 and August 18.

 Mars retrogrades in Aquarius from June 26 until August 13 in your house of letting go and past lives. Since it is also the house of hospitals, please drive slowly and don't be on your phone while walking in the street (or driving). Since it is also the house of hidden enemies, you might encounter antagonism from certain people who you thought were your friends. From August 13 to August 27, Mars is retrograding in your house of friends, communities, and governments. As you can see, reassessing your relationships with friends, groups, and organizations is a major theme in 2018. There might be some conflict or strife within your social circles. Try to stay out of other people's wars.

In September, once Mars goes direct, a great deal of projects that were held back will start flowing. You will feel more energized and optimistic. It will be a good time to assume a leadership position in your company or start new projects.

PISCES ♓

Venus: Money and Love

Venus is the ruler of comfort, luxury, finance, talents, values, art, and relationships. She is also associated with Maat, the goddess of justice and law.

Venus works in beauty cycles: the more you love yourself, the more you believe in yourself. The better your self-image, the more you connect to your talents. The more you develop and invest in your talent, the more money you can make. Venus message is: love yourself and money will follow. Some, however, think that the more money they make, the more they would love themselves and that is a mistake. This year during Venus retrograde (October 6 – November 16), you will be able to change your attitude and fix your relationship to money.

Venus is in your sign between February 10 and March 6, making you far more attractive to others. It is a great time for romance, making money, and connecting to your artistic side. This is a good time for you to rebrand yourself, dress differently, change your hair, get some new clothes. Not a bad time to indulge and pamper yourself (as long as it is healthy and does not harm you or anyone else).

This year, Venus will retrograde between October 6 and November 16. First, Venus retrogrades in Scorpio (October 6 – 31), and then she will retrograde in Libra between October 31 and November 16. When Venus is retrograding in Scorpio, it can affect your relationship with foreigners and multinational corporations. If you plan to travel around that time, take extra care how you deal with people abroad. You might be tempted to lie or bend the truth to save a relationship, but it is not a good idea. When Venus retrogrades in Libra, it can create challenges but also profound lessons in relationships and partnerships, especially with intimate or sexual relationships as Venus retrogrades in your house of death and sexuality. There might be some issues with inheritance or your partner's finance.

Conclusion:

This year, your new year resolution should be around friendship and your connection to companies, clients, or the government. Saturn can help manifest many changes in your social circles. It is a year of travel and exploration, a year when you might feel called upon to journey in distant lands. 2018 is the year where you can reshape your philosophy and feel authentic and real. This year, you become a teacher who learns and a student who teaches.

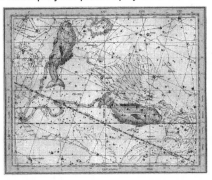

PISCES ♓

65717947R00115

Made in the USA
San Bernardino, CA
04 January 2018